MANUAL OF LETTERING

MANUAL
OF
LETTERING

BY

CECIL WADE, F.R.S.A.

Author of "Modern Lettering and Layout," "Lettering for Amateurs," etc.

BLANDFORD PRESS

16 WEST CENTRAL STREET, LONDON, W.C.1

First Published 1952

Made and Printed in Great Britain at the Pitman Press, Bath, and published by
Blandford Press Ltd., 16 West Central Street, London, W.C.1

Contents

Introduction

My purpose in preparing by hand all the plates which appear in this book—and this was a formidable task—was not just to present the various alphabets in an unorthodox manner, but because extensive experience in teaching lettering has convinced me that a great deal can be learned by studying the letters separately in their various forms or "faces" in relation to each other rather than in alphabetical form. Many complete alphabets, however excellently represented on one page, are too small to enable the student to appreciate the many subtleties of letter design. I have therefore presented the letters large enough for detailed study and varied their sizes according to the amount of interest and study required. Such study and analysis is important if the reason for each design is to be appreciated.

It will be seen therefore that my purpose was not only to illustrate the styles of lettering but also to help the student in the appreciation of letter design and so develop his ability to become a letter craftsman and designer. Had I presented the complete alphabets on a double-page it would still have reduced the size of the letters and made analytical study impossible. To draw them larger, with the alphabets occupying more pages would have proved tedious in finding a particular style. Whereas in the manner presented, any letter of the style illustrated can be found on the appropriate pages. There will inevitably be a certain amount of searching but, I do feel this particular manner of presentation is very good as it should prove more stimulating and instructive than looking through complete alphabets one after the other.

In this mode of presentation I have been largely influenced by my own index card reference of lettering which has been built up over a period of years. This reference is made up in groups, not alphabets, similar to the arrangement in this book. In producing this book I hope that the system which has been of practical use in my own case, will prove a useful and helpful reference for the reader.

LONDON   CECIL WADE
February, 1952

NEULAND

Beton

FALSTAFF

Ultra Bodoni Italic

CASLON
OLD FACE
Italic

COOPER BLACK

MEMPHIS

SLIM BLACK

Winter SALE

GILL SANS SHADOW

CINEMA

PLAYBILL

Gothic

Pen

ROMAN

GILL

SANS

Sans Condensed

It's Exciting

Look!

Fashions

POSTER

1 2 3 4 5 6

7 8 9 0 &

1 2 3 4 5 6 7
8 9 0 & 7

1 2 3 4 5 6

7 8 9 0 & £

1234 56 7890 £

1 2 3 4 5 6 7 8 9 0 & £

1 2 3 4 5 6 7 8 9 0 & £

1 2 3 4 5 6 7 8 9 0 & £

1 2 3 4 5 6
7 8 9 0 & £

1 2 3 4 5 6
7 8 9 0 & £

1 2 3 4 5 6 7
8 9 0 & £

1 2 3 4 5 6
7 8 9 & £

1234567890 O&£

1234567890 &£

1234567890 &£

1234567890 &£

1234567
890 O & £

1234567
890 & £

123456
7890&£

1234567
890 £ &

1 2 3 4 5 6
7 8 9 0

1 2 3 4 5 6
7 8 9 & £

1 2 3 4 5 6 7
8 9 0 & £

1 2 3 4 5 6
7 8 9 0 & £

Aa Aa Aa

Aa A

Aa aa

Aa A

Aa Aa Aa

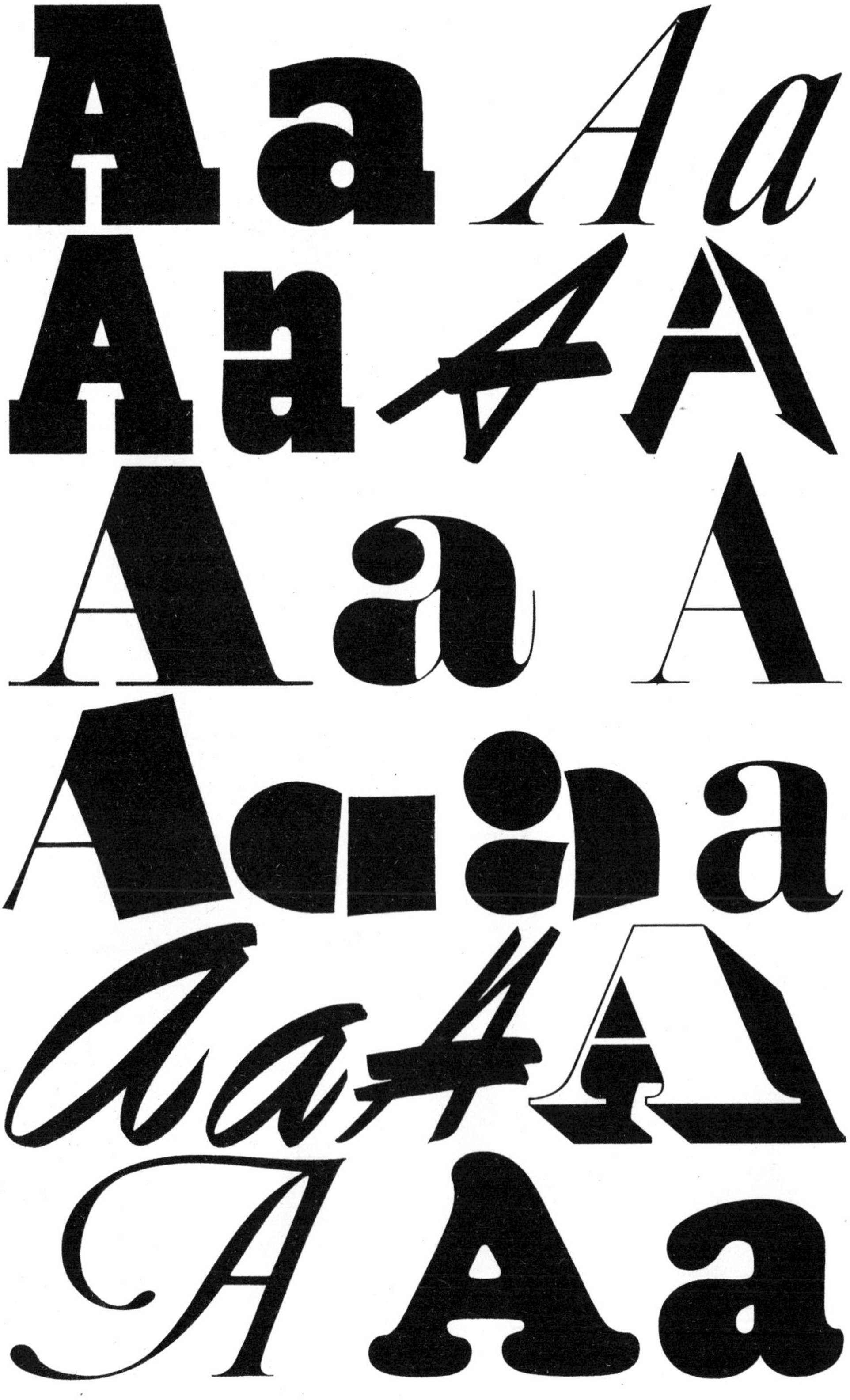

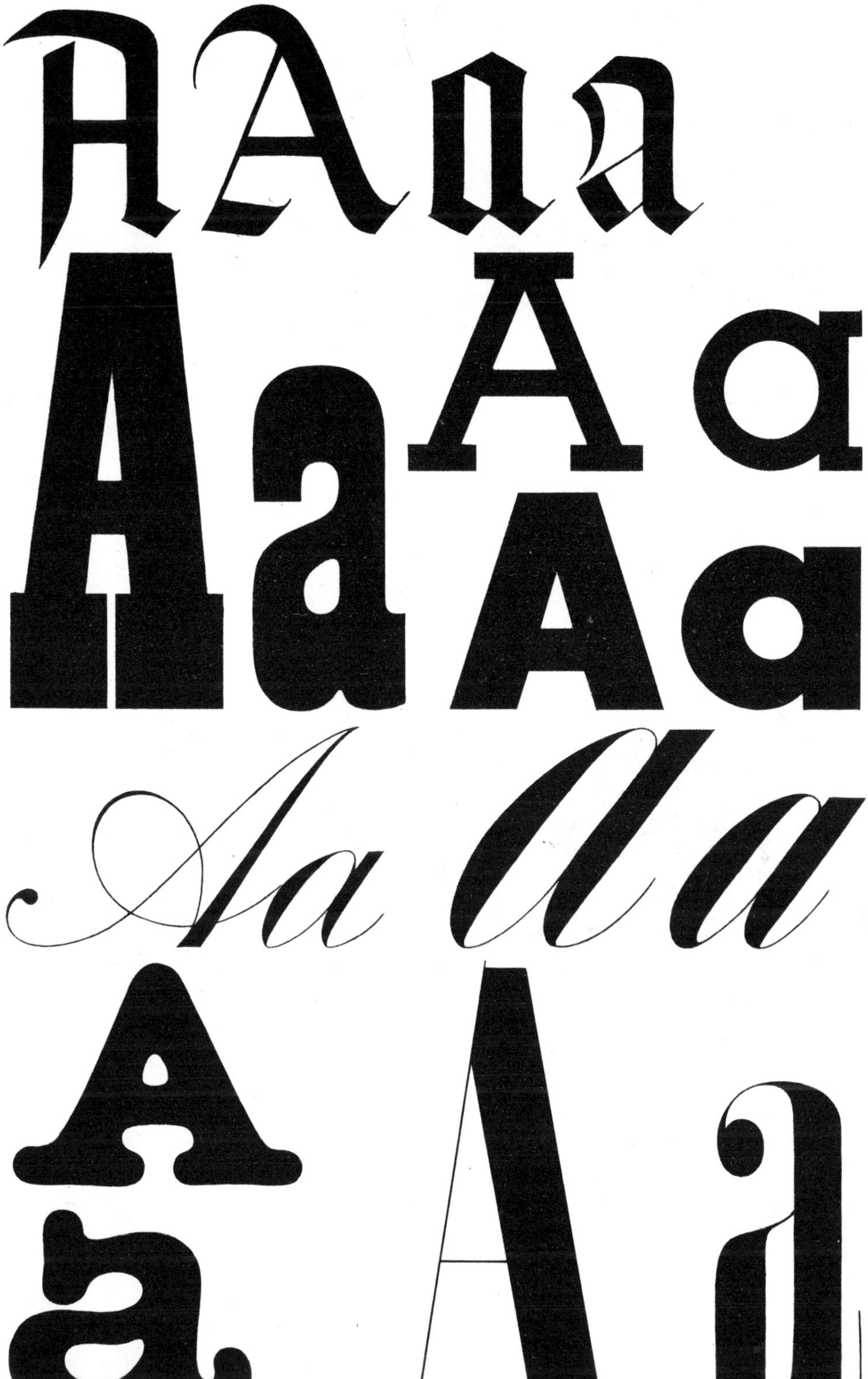

Вь Вь В

Вее

В

В Вь Вь Вь

Вь Вь Вь

ВЬ *ВЬ* *Вb*

Вb *Вb* *вb* В

Вb В b
Вb
В b
Вb В b

Вb В b
Вb Вb

Bb Bbb

B B B B

B

Bb Bb

Bbb Bb

Bb Bb

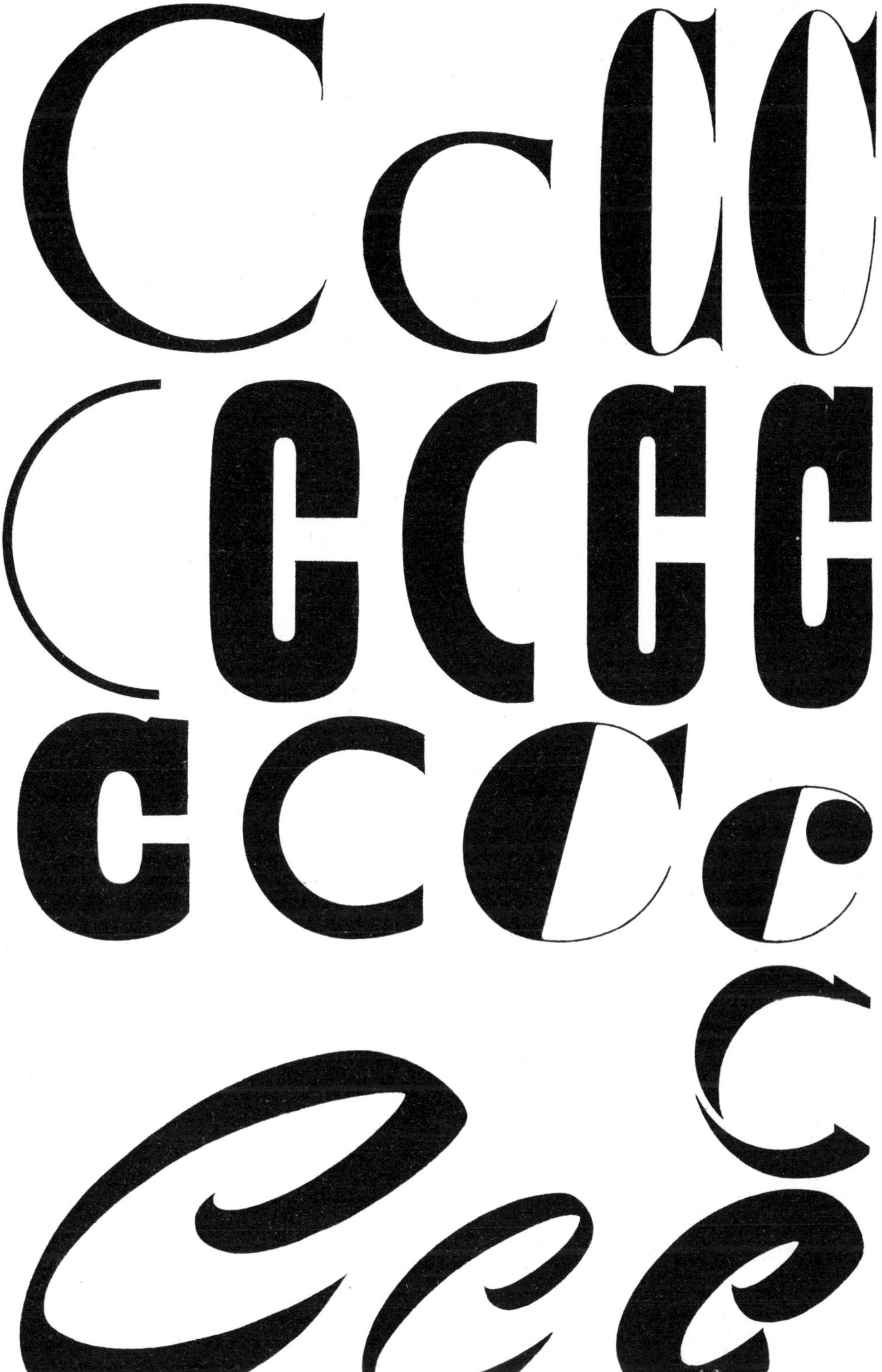

C c C c C c C c

C C C C C

C Court

Cinema

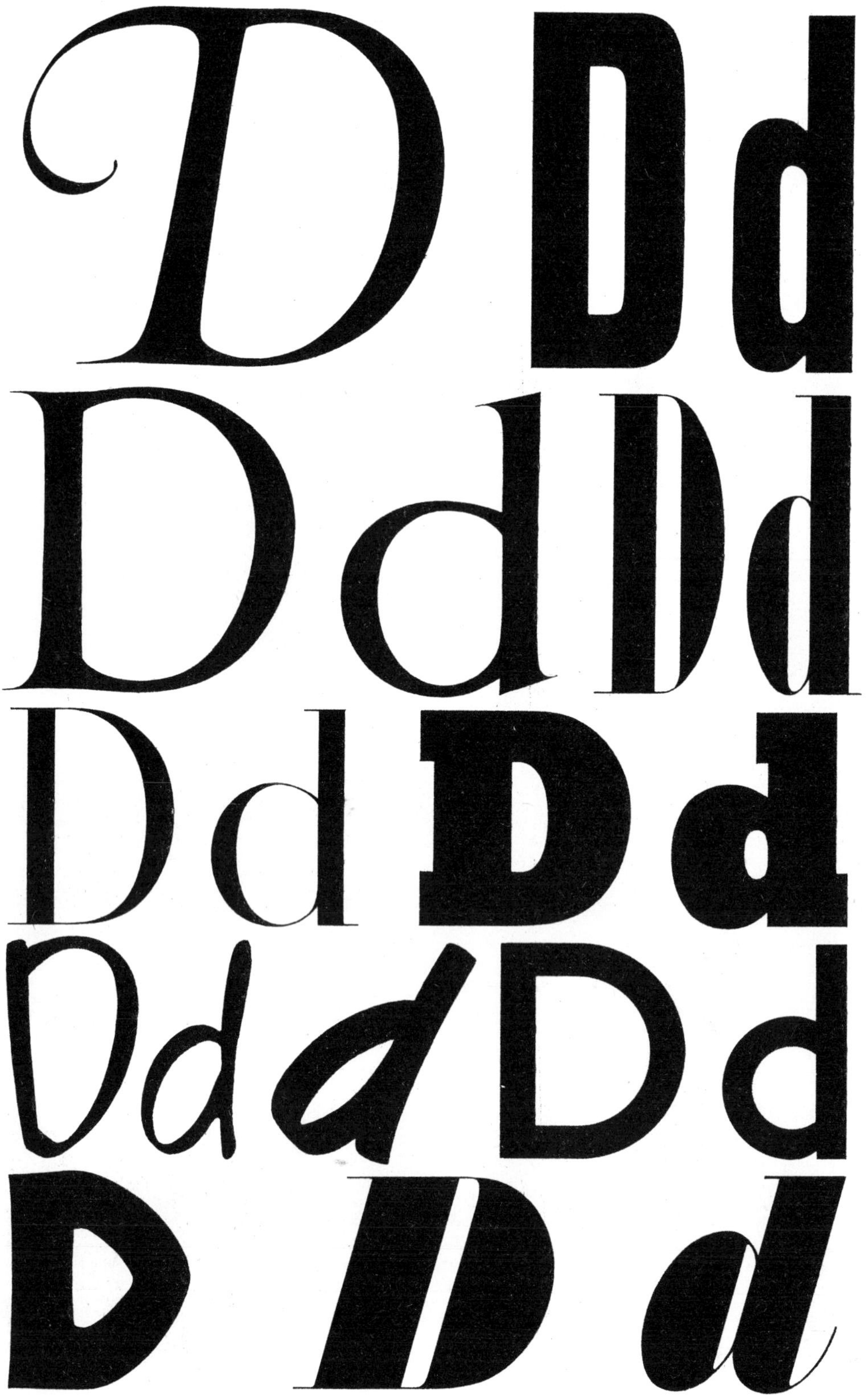

Dd DD D
Dd D Dd D
Dd Dd D
Dd Dd d
Dd Dd d
Dd Dd D

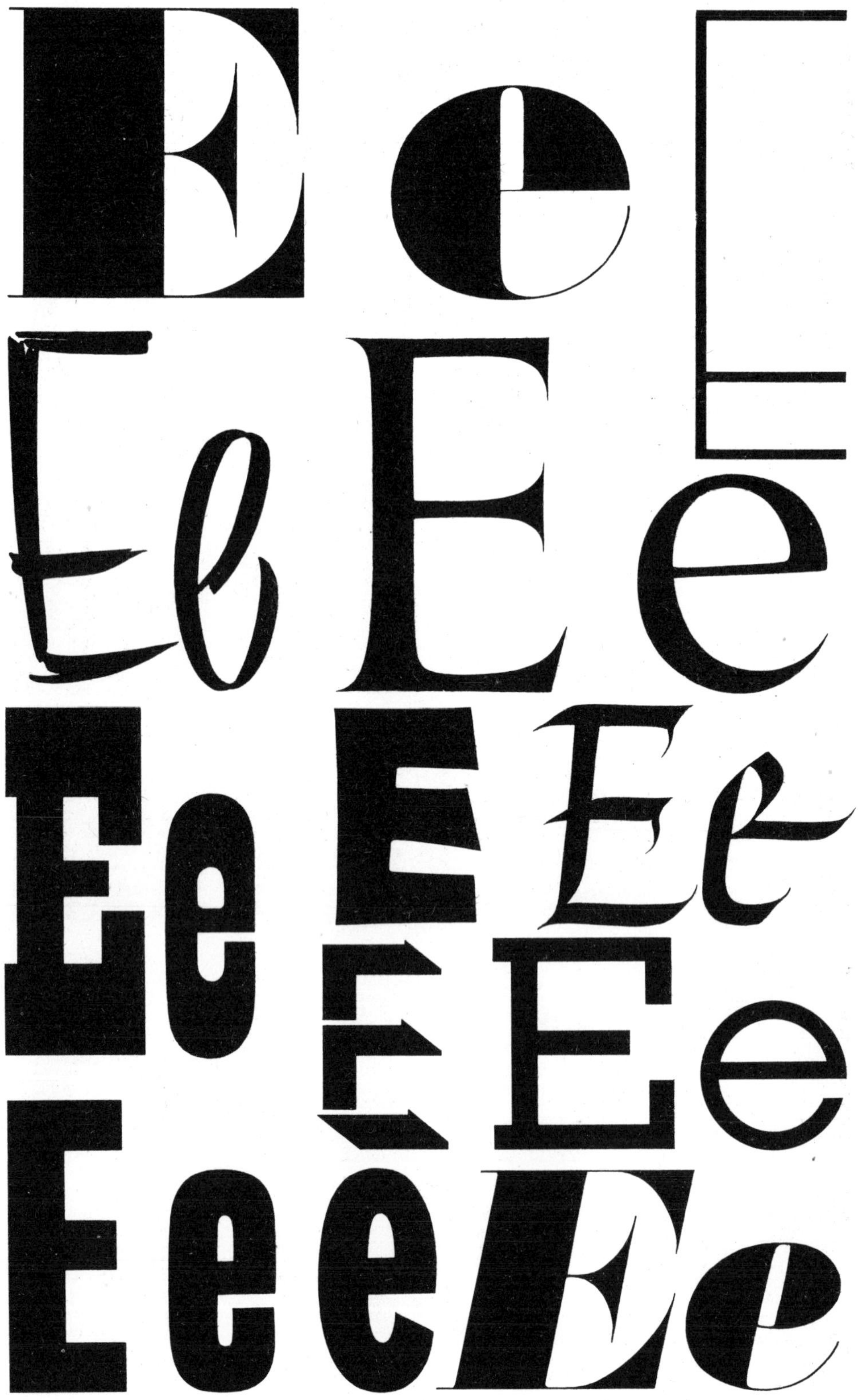

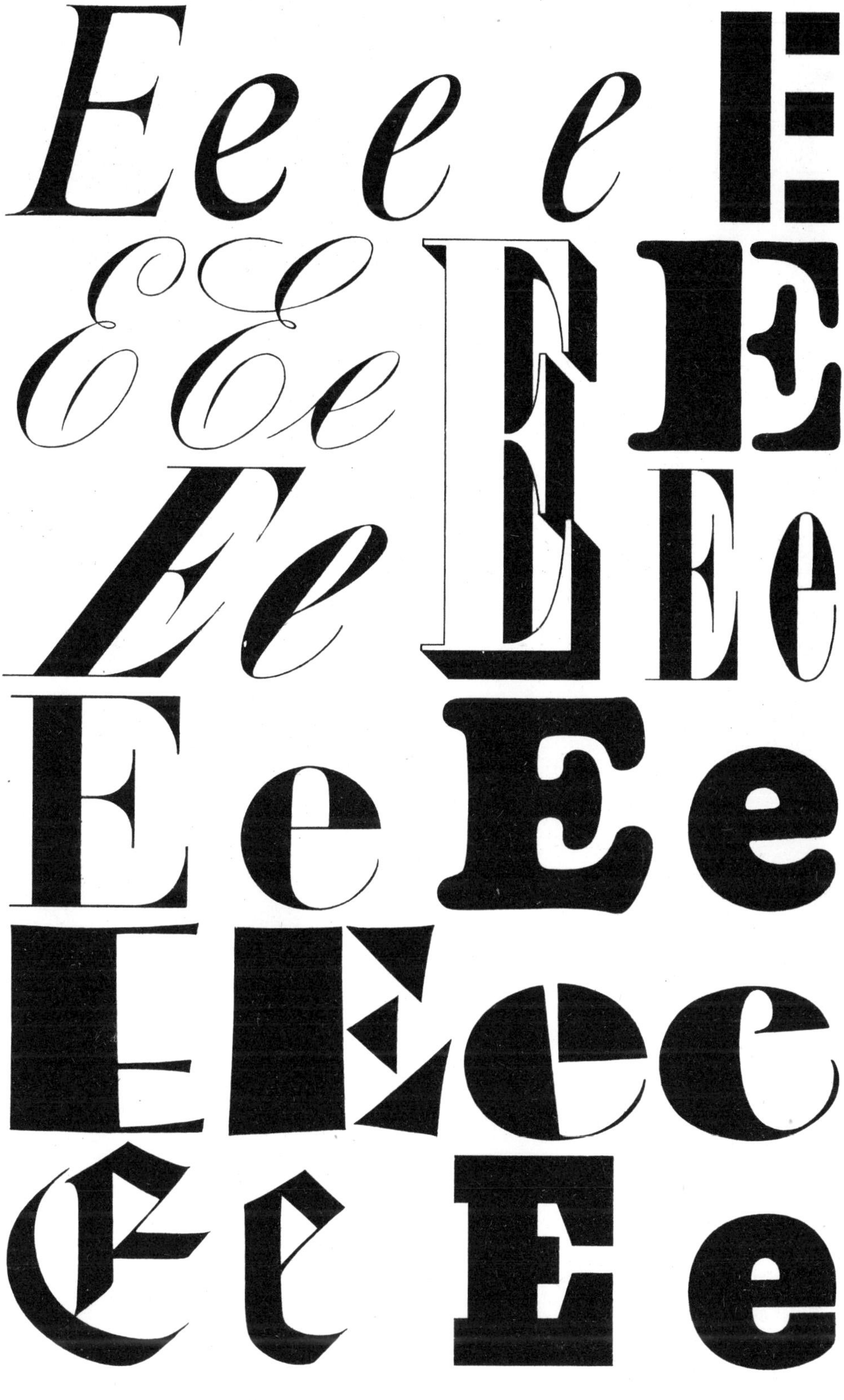

EeEe

EGRET

Ece ≡

Enter Now

EASTWOODS

E e E e

East

Easier Shave

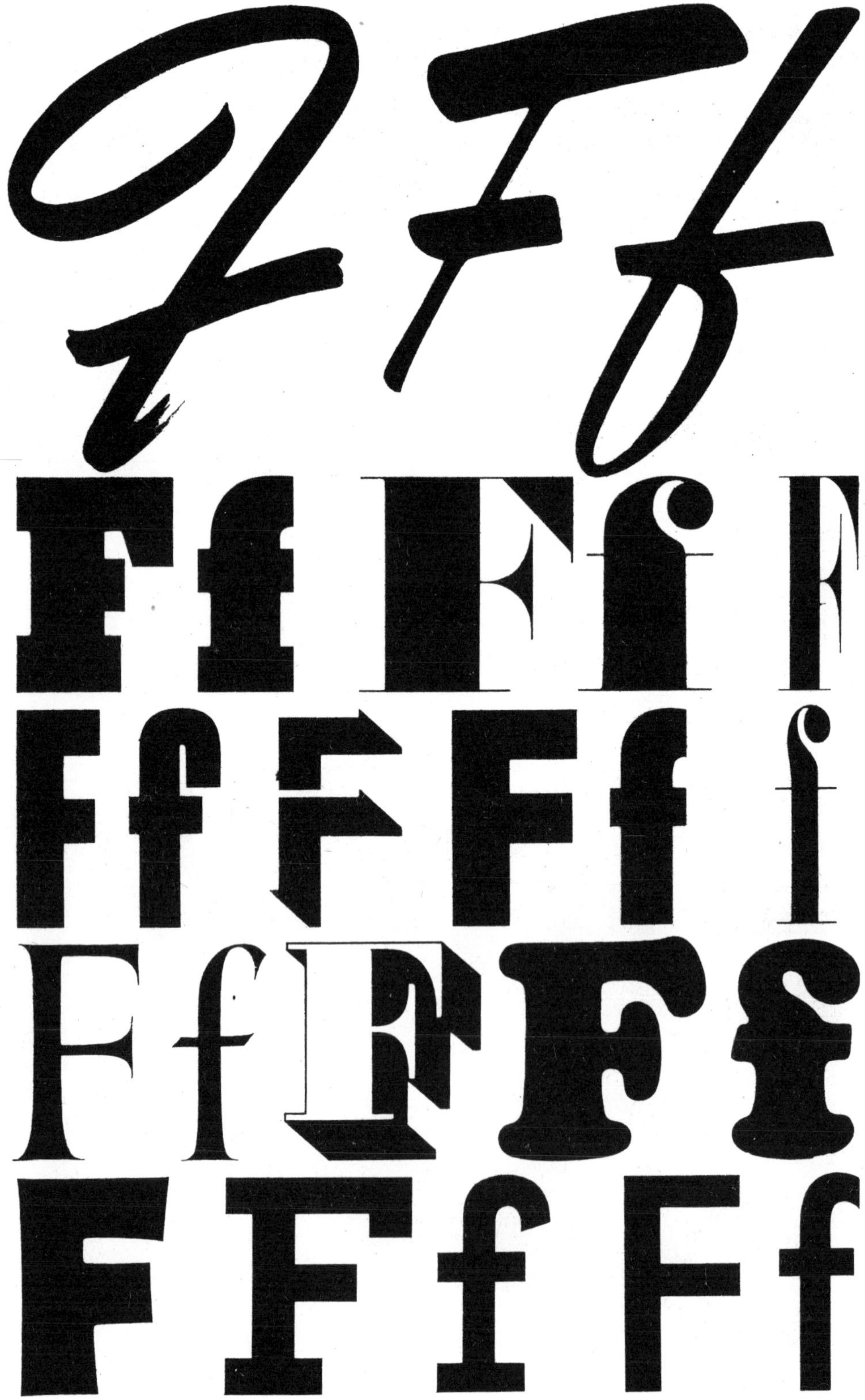

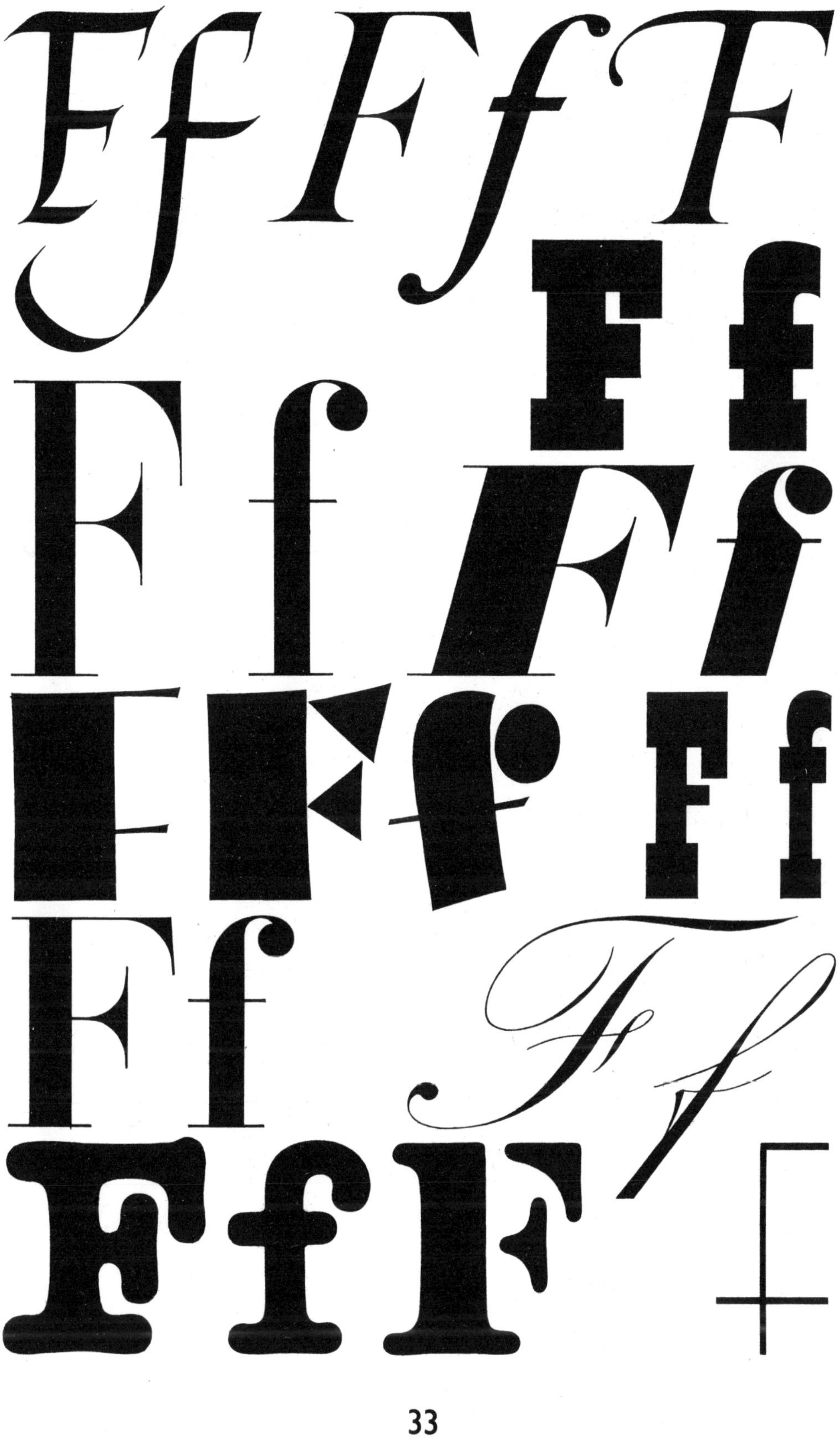

FfF

focus on food

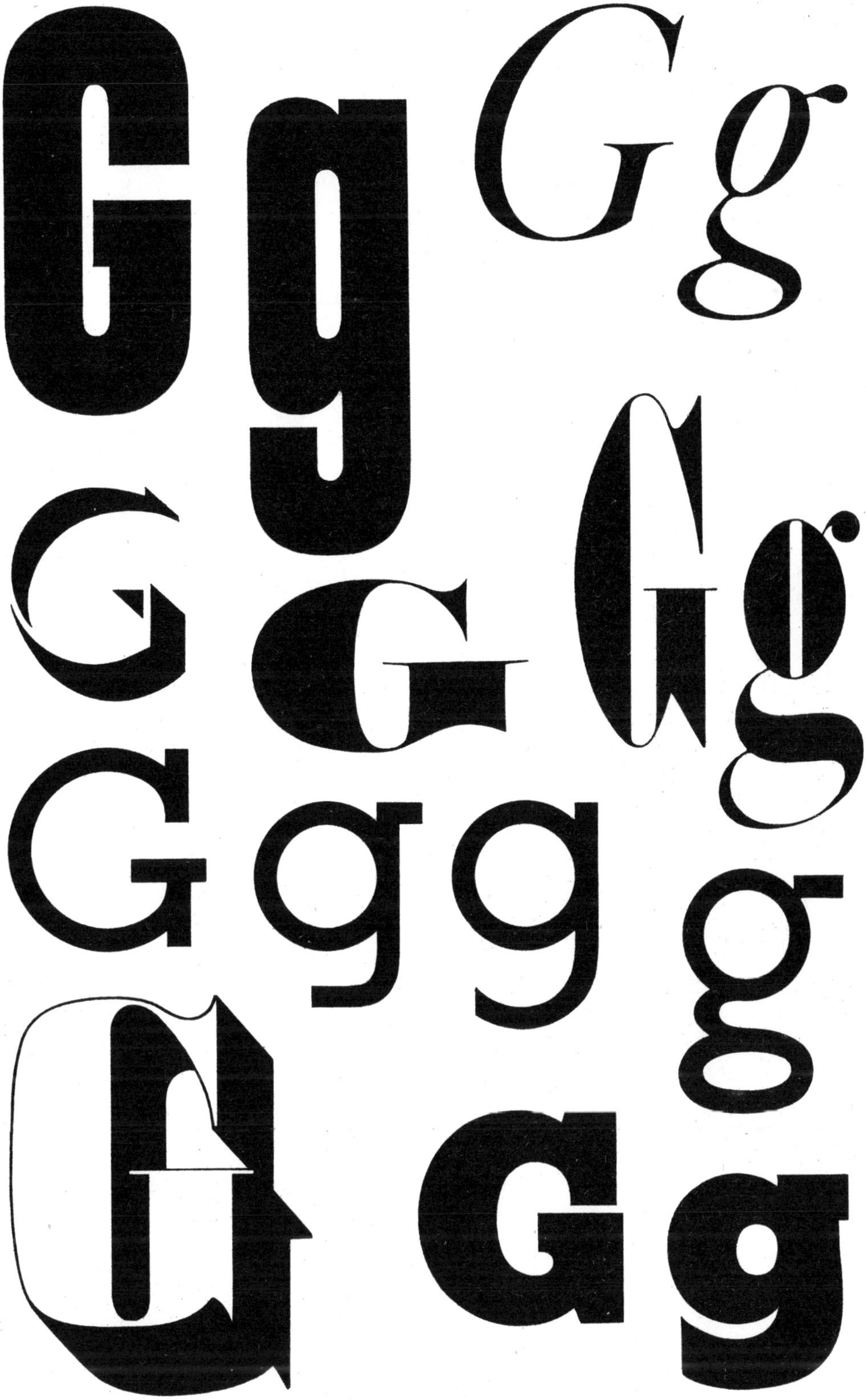

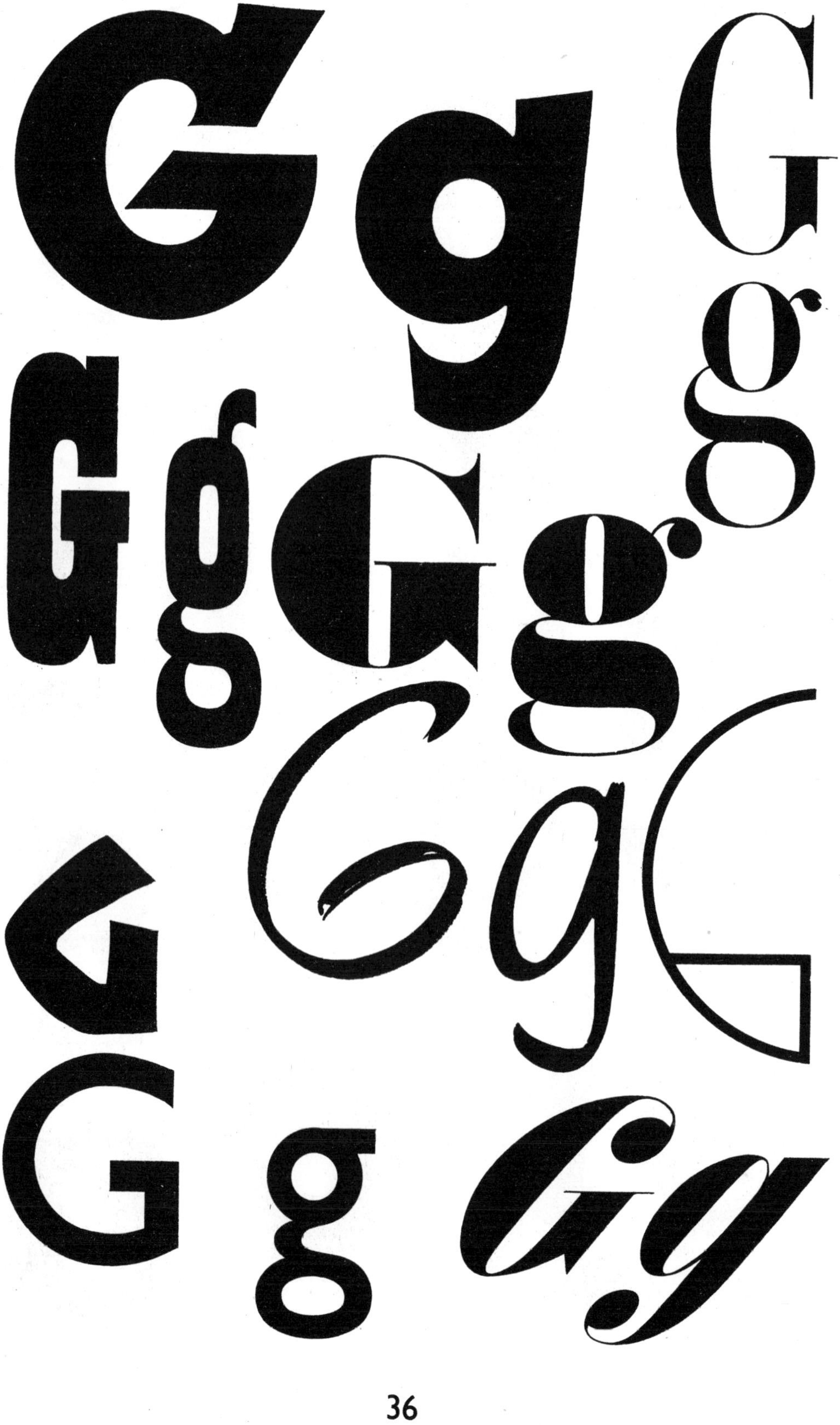

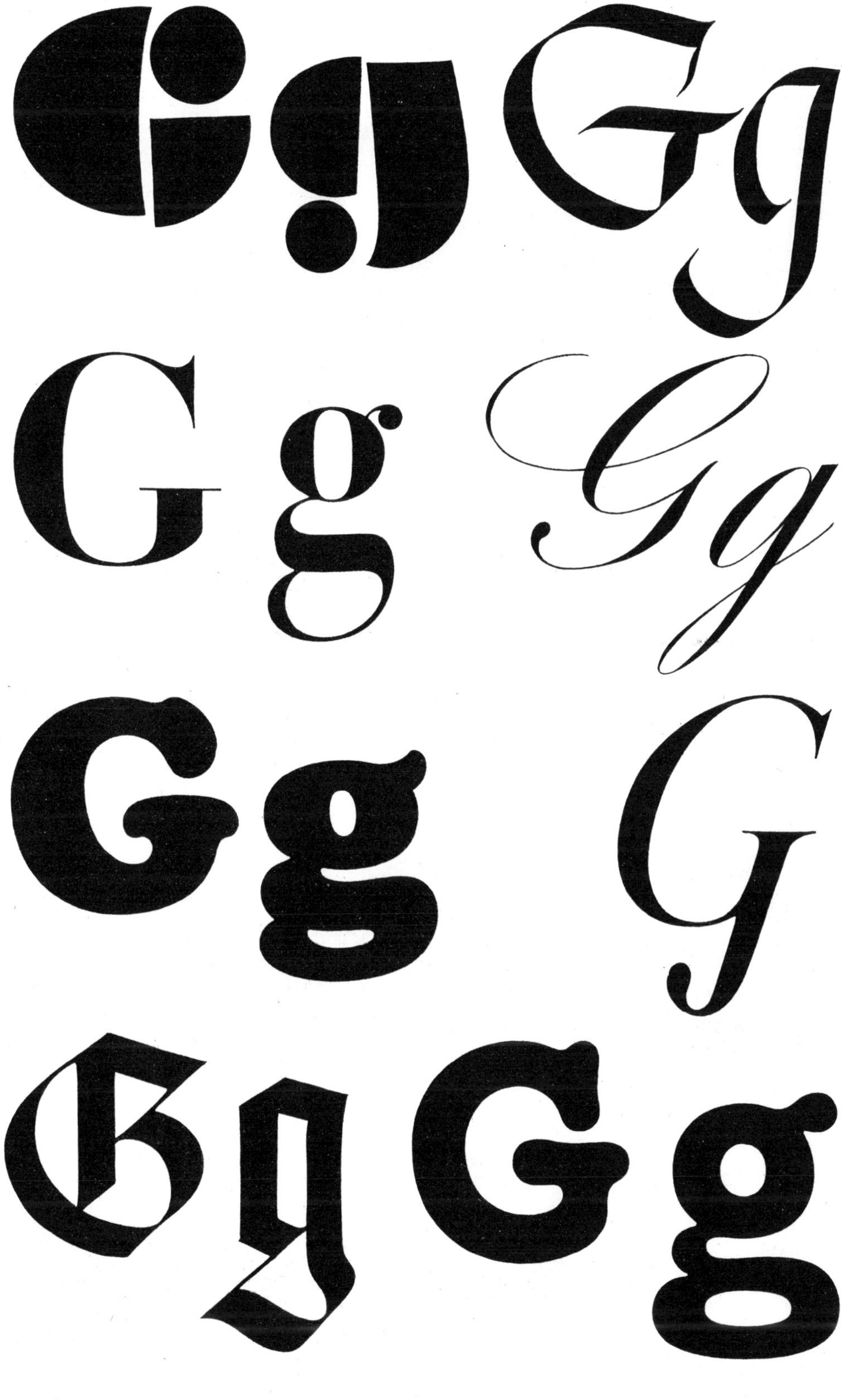

Gg

Garden

Great
News

Hh Hh Hh
Hh Hh Hh
Hh Hh Hh
Hh Hh Hh
Hh Hh Hh

Hh Hh H-H

HhHh *Hh*

HbHh

Hh *Hh hh*

H *Hh*

H h h h
Hh H
Hh H
Hh
Hh
Hh
H h
Hello Hh

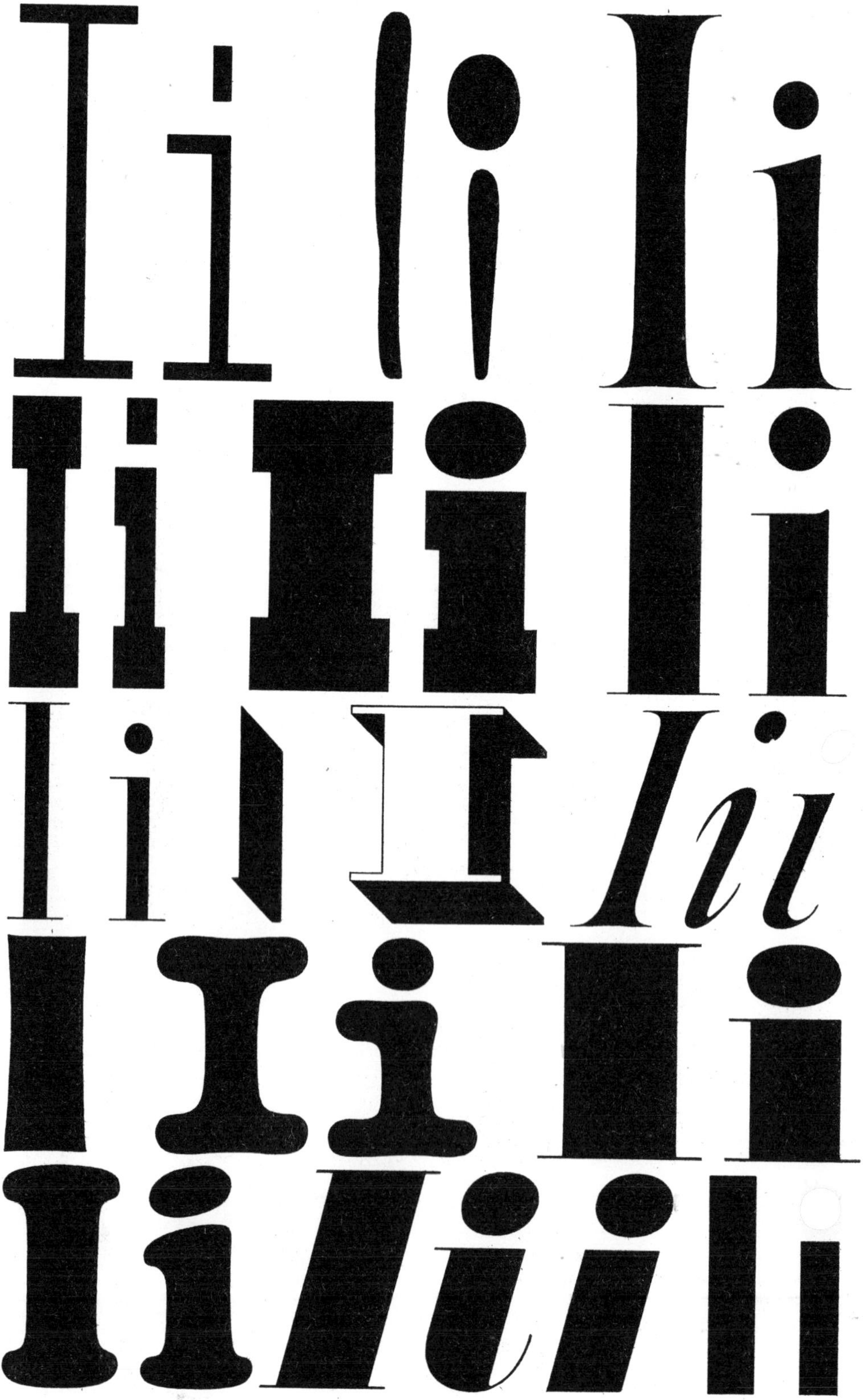

I i Ii Ii Ii
Ii Ii Ii Ii
Ji Ii

Ices

J j J j J

J j J j J j

J j J j

J j J j

JJ jj Jj

Jj Jj Jj

JUNE

Jumper

46

K k k k
K k · K k
K k K k
K k · k
K k k k

Kk Kk
Kk Kk
Kk Kk
Kk Kk
Kk Kk
Kk Kk

KKKK
KKKKK
K
Kk
Klondyke

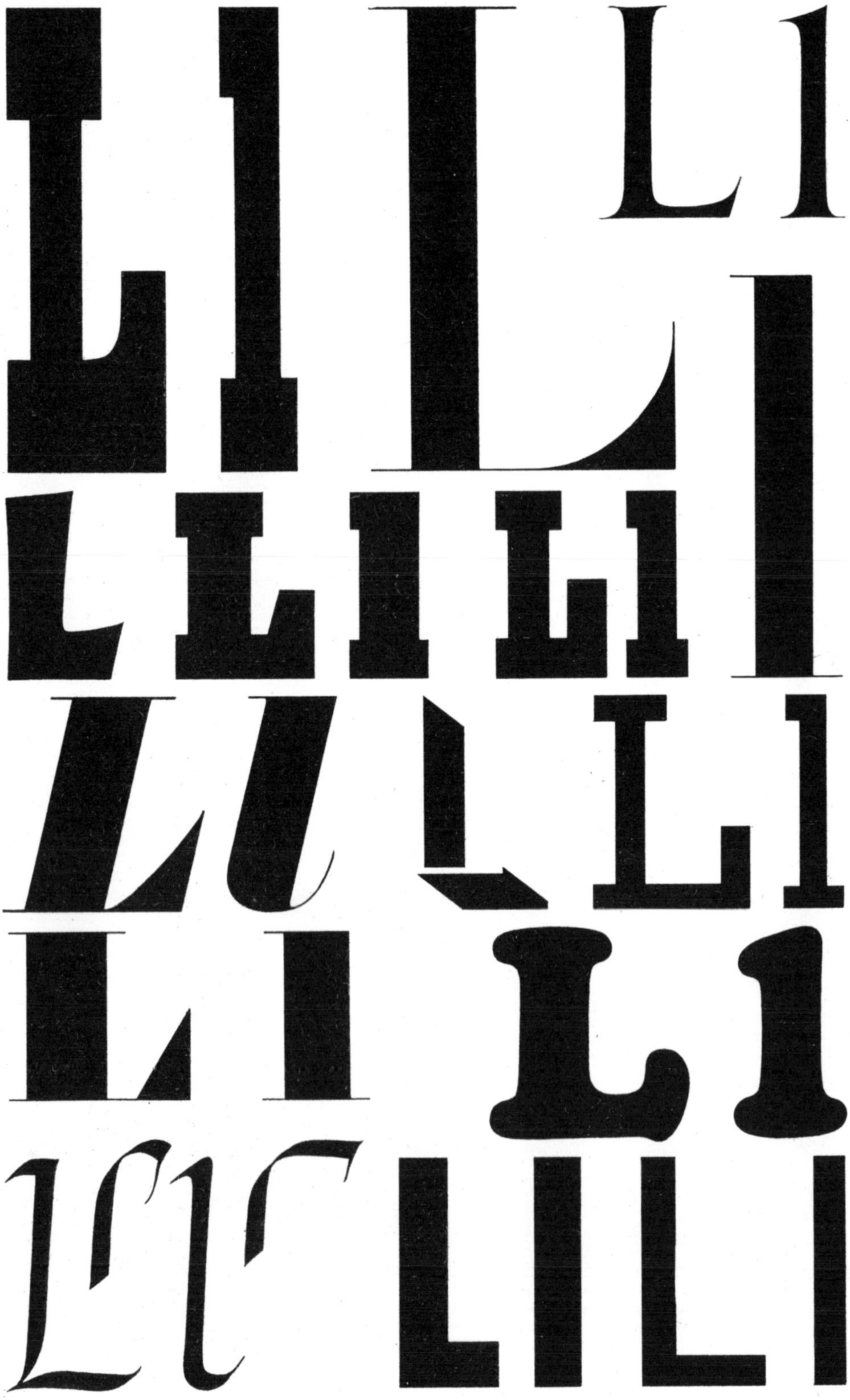
Ll L Ll
l
Ll Ll Ll
Ll Ll Ll
Ll Ll
Ll LlLl

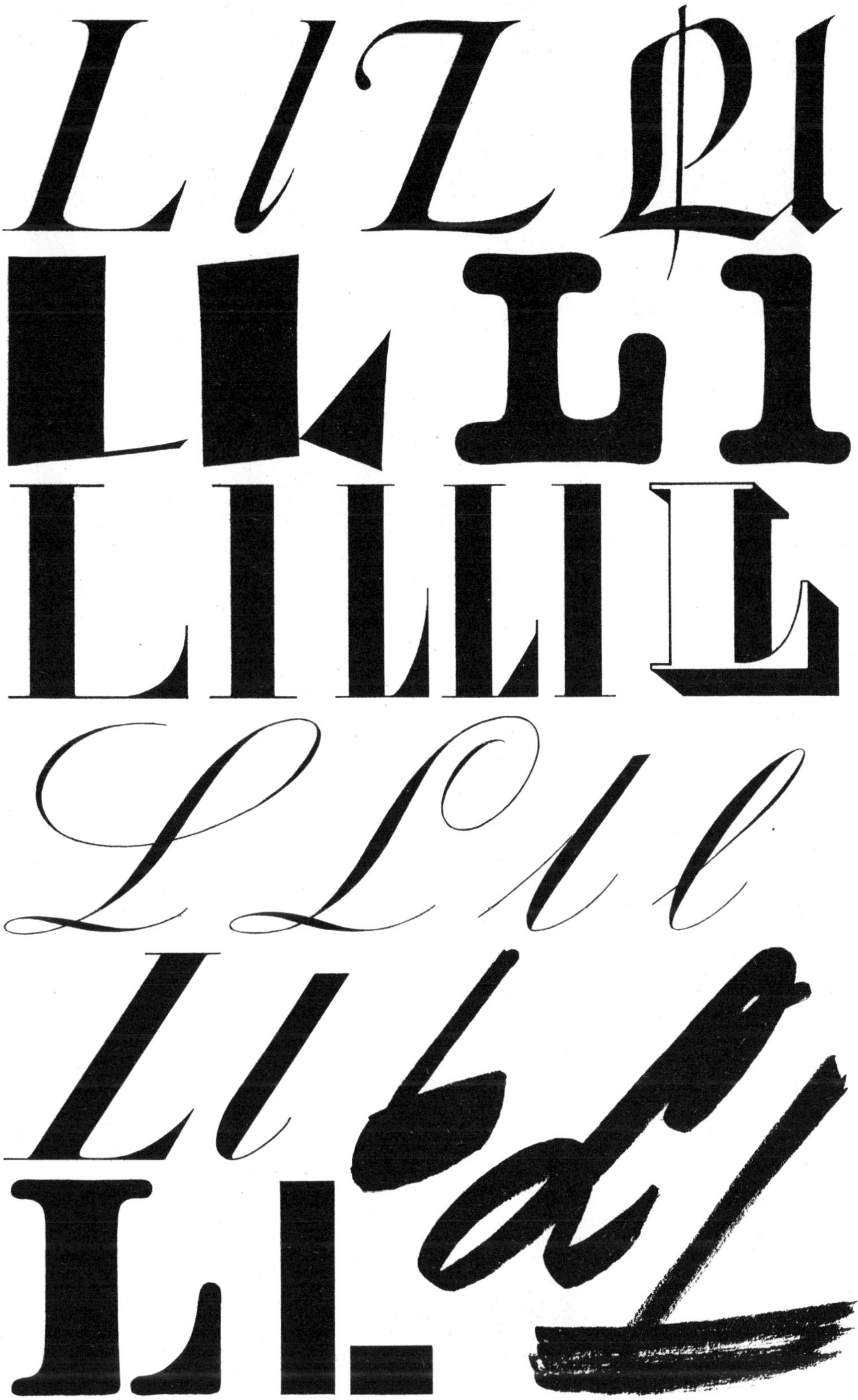

M m
M M m
M M M m
m m M M
M M M m

M m M m

M m M

M m M

M m M

M m M

M m M

MMm
MmmM
MmMm
MMm
MMm
MMm

M m

M . M

M m N

Merry

Xmas

Nn Nn Nn
Nn Nn
Nn Nn
Nn Nn
Nn Nn
Nn Nn

N N
N N n
N N N n
N N n N n
N N n N n

N N n
N Nn N
Nn Nn
Naive
NN

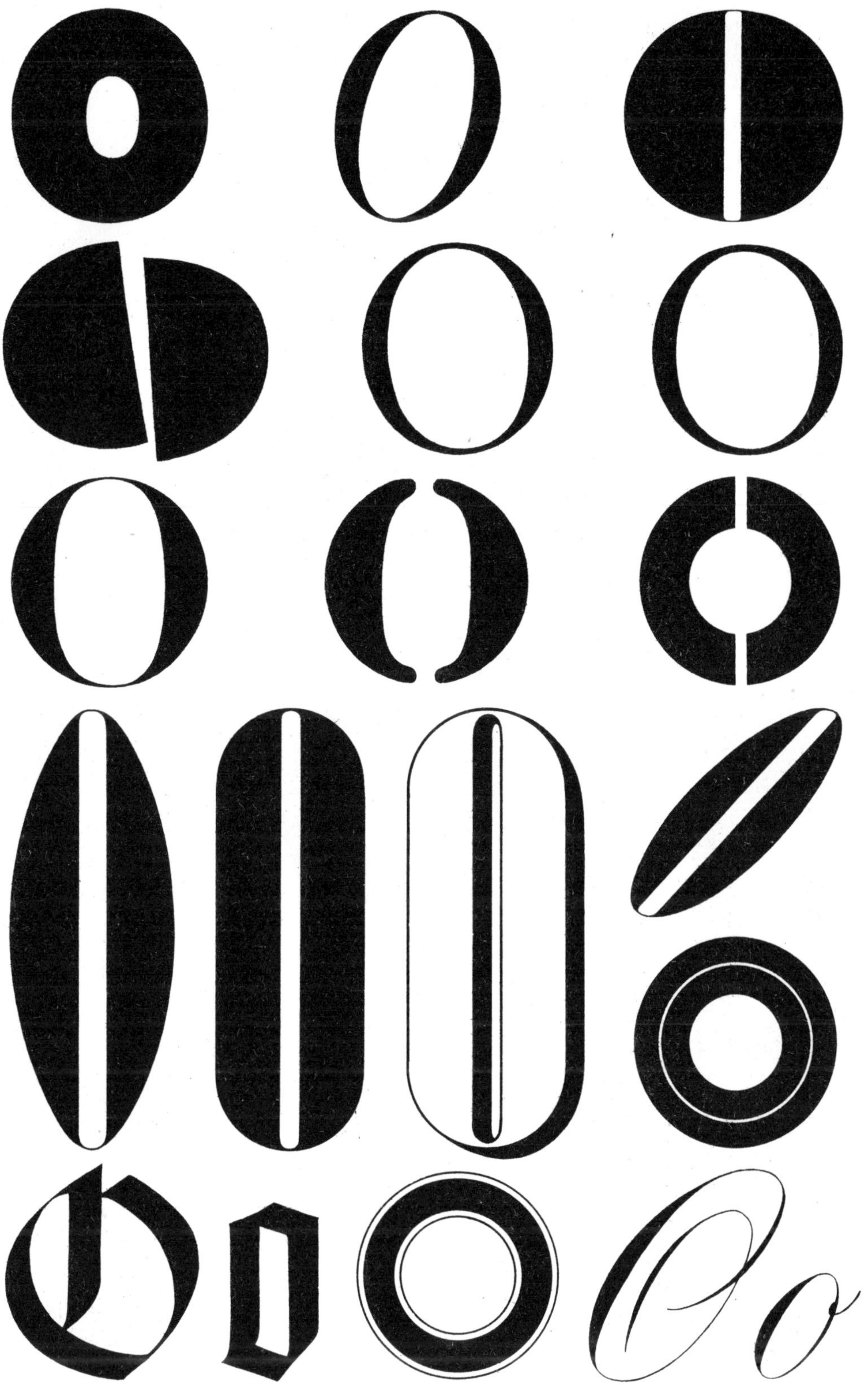

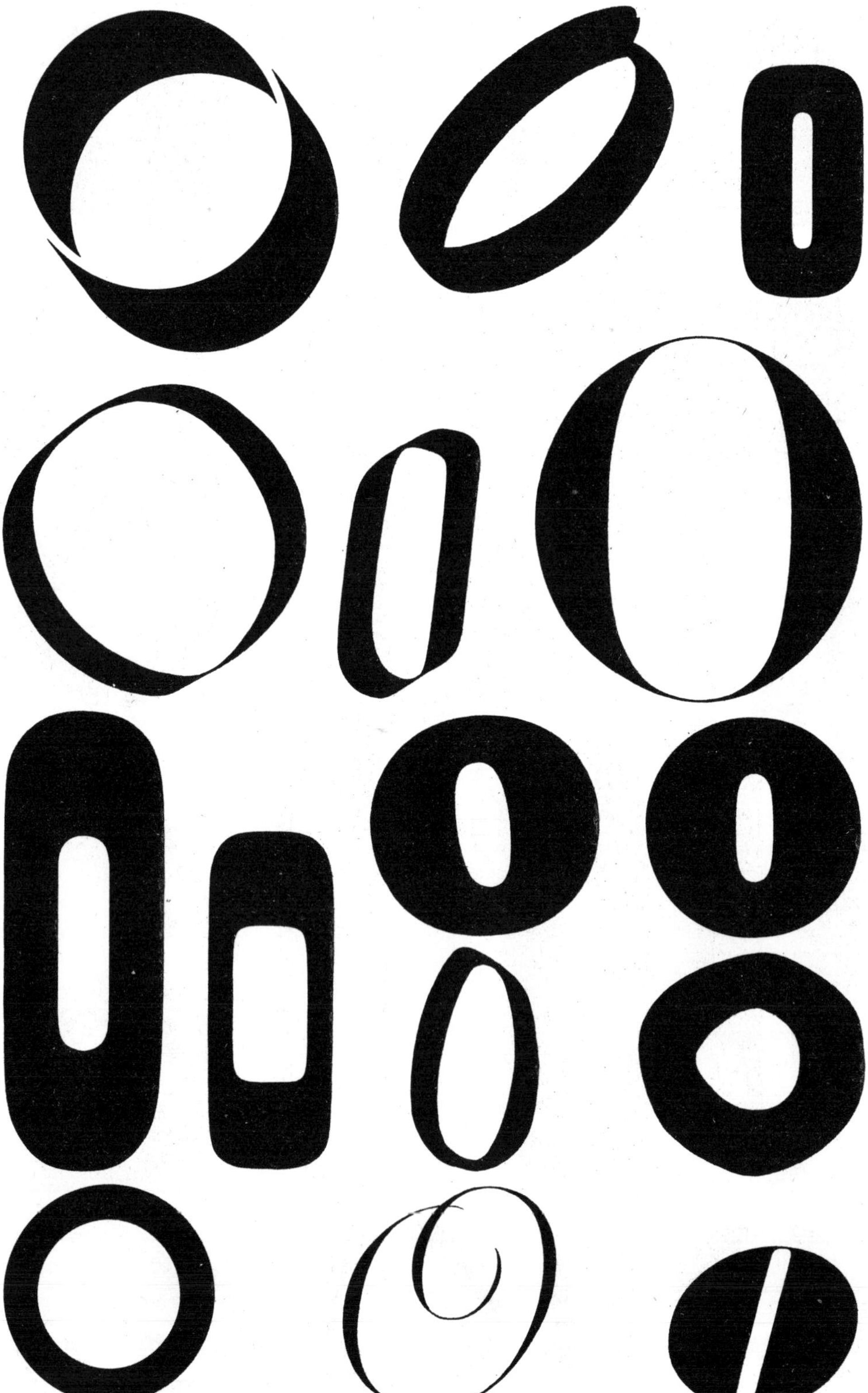

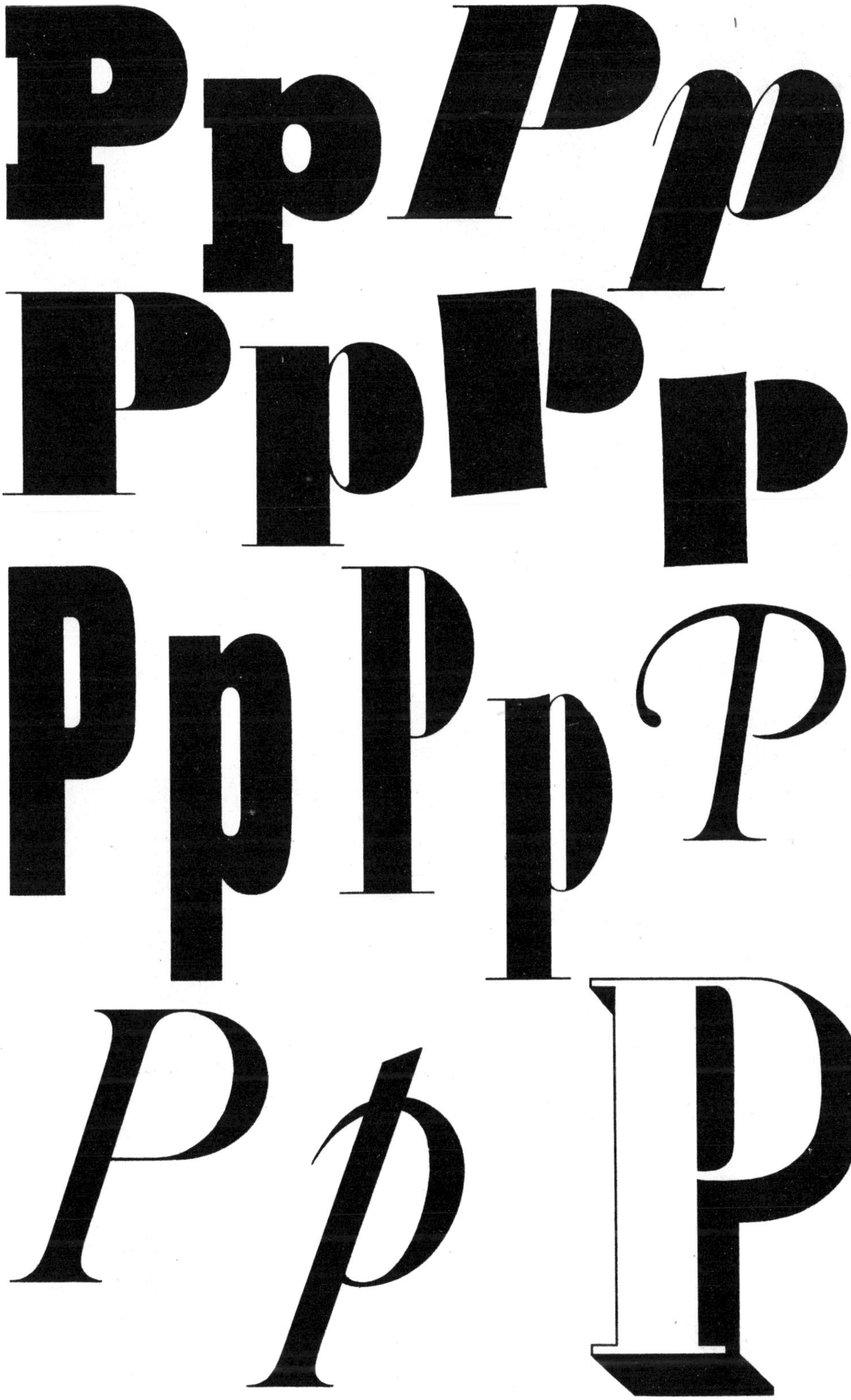

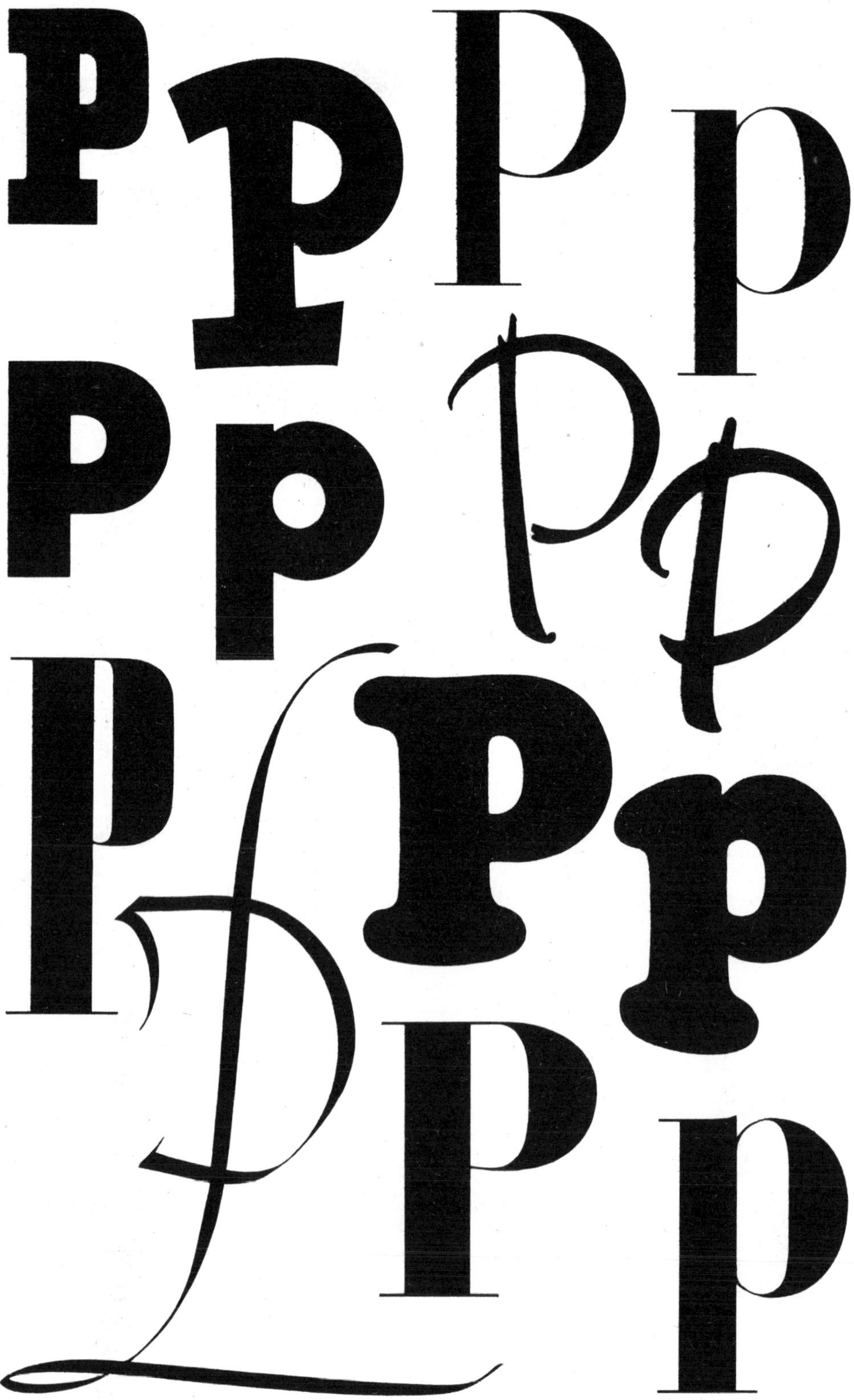

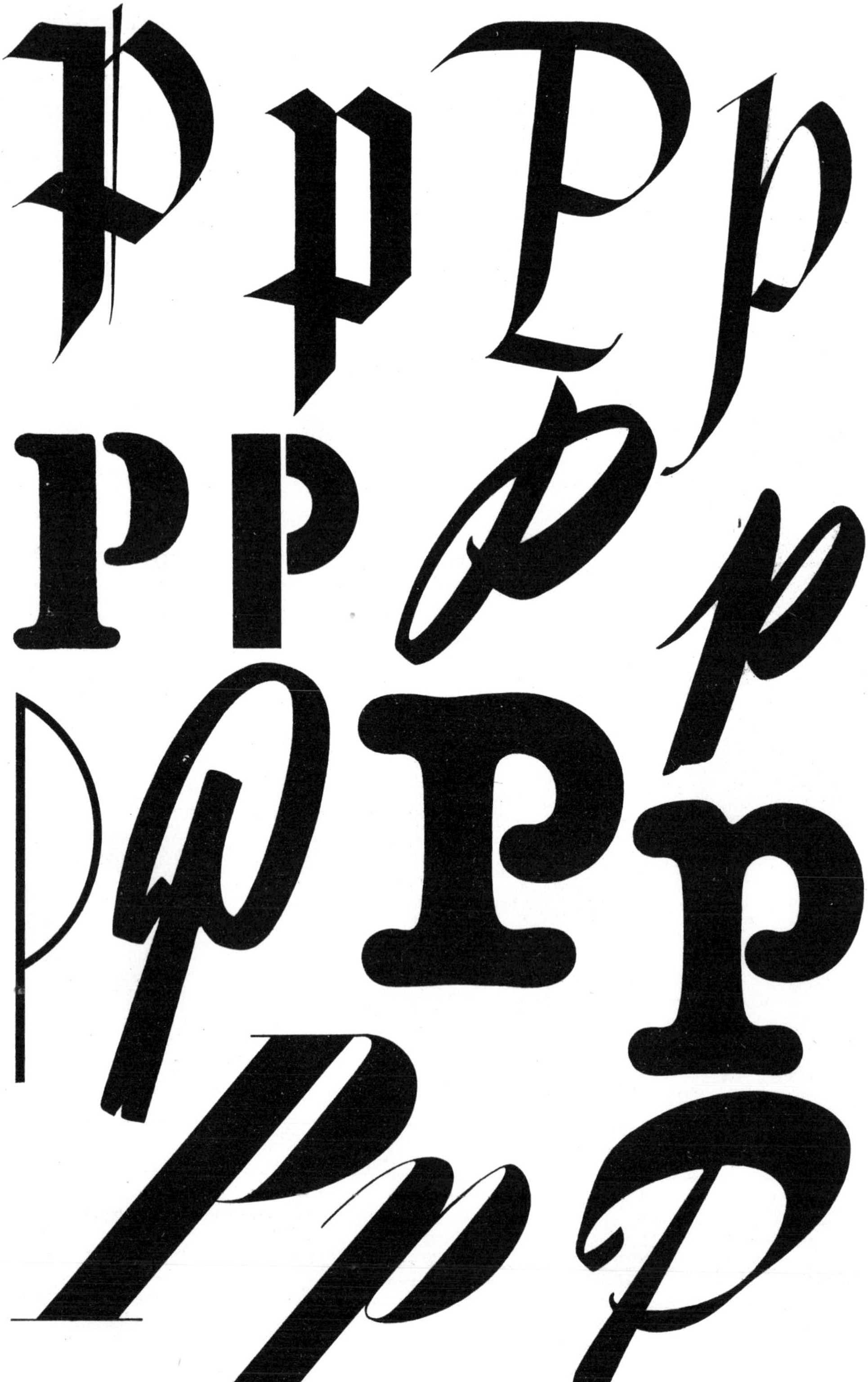

P p
Poetry

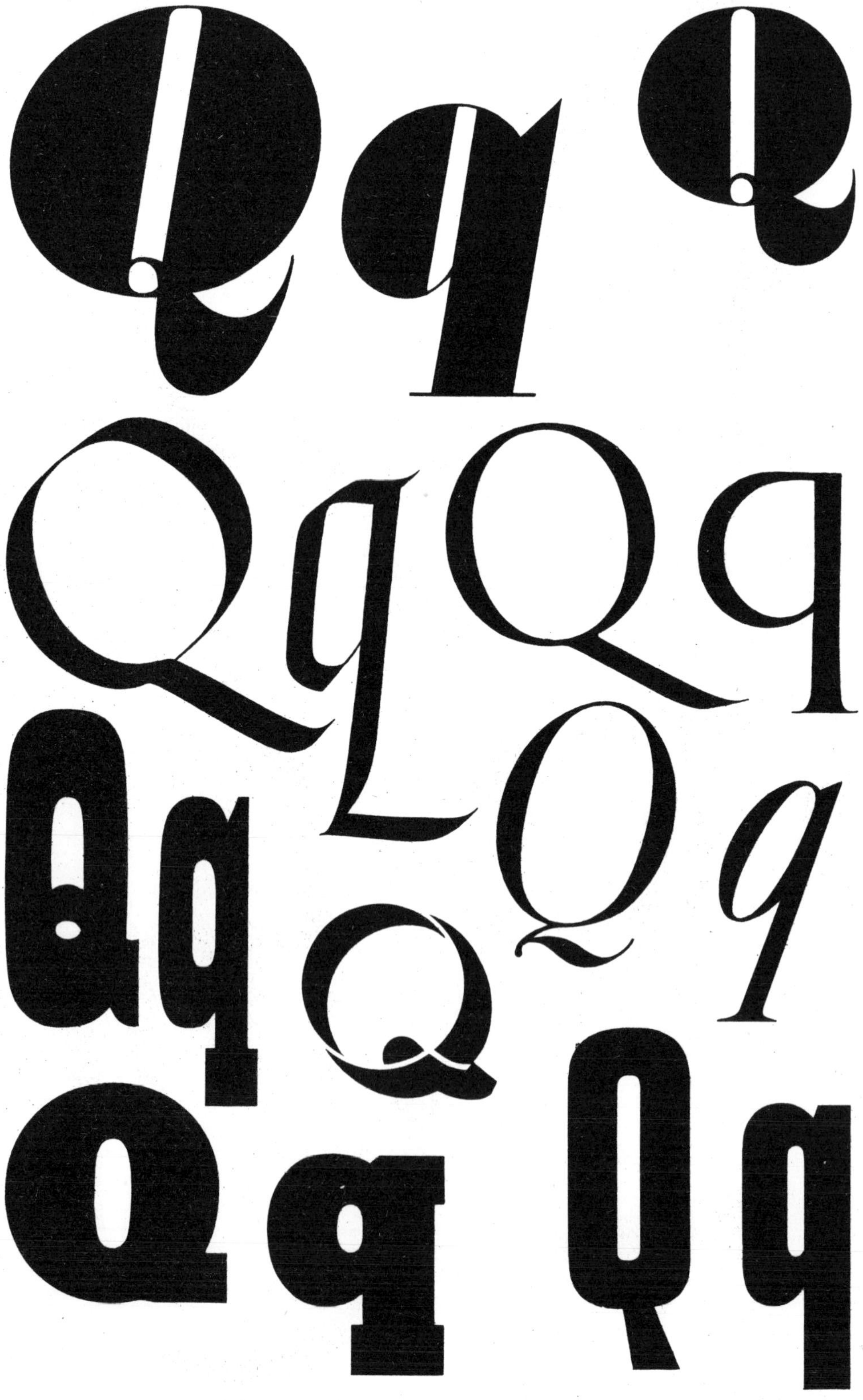

Q q Q
Q q Q
2 q Q q
Q q Q q

Qq Qq

Qq Qq

2 Qq

Qq q

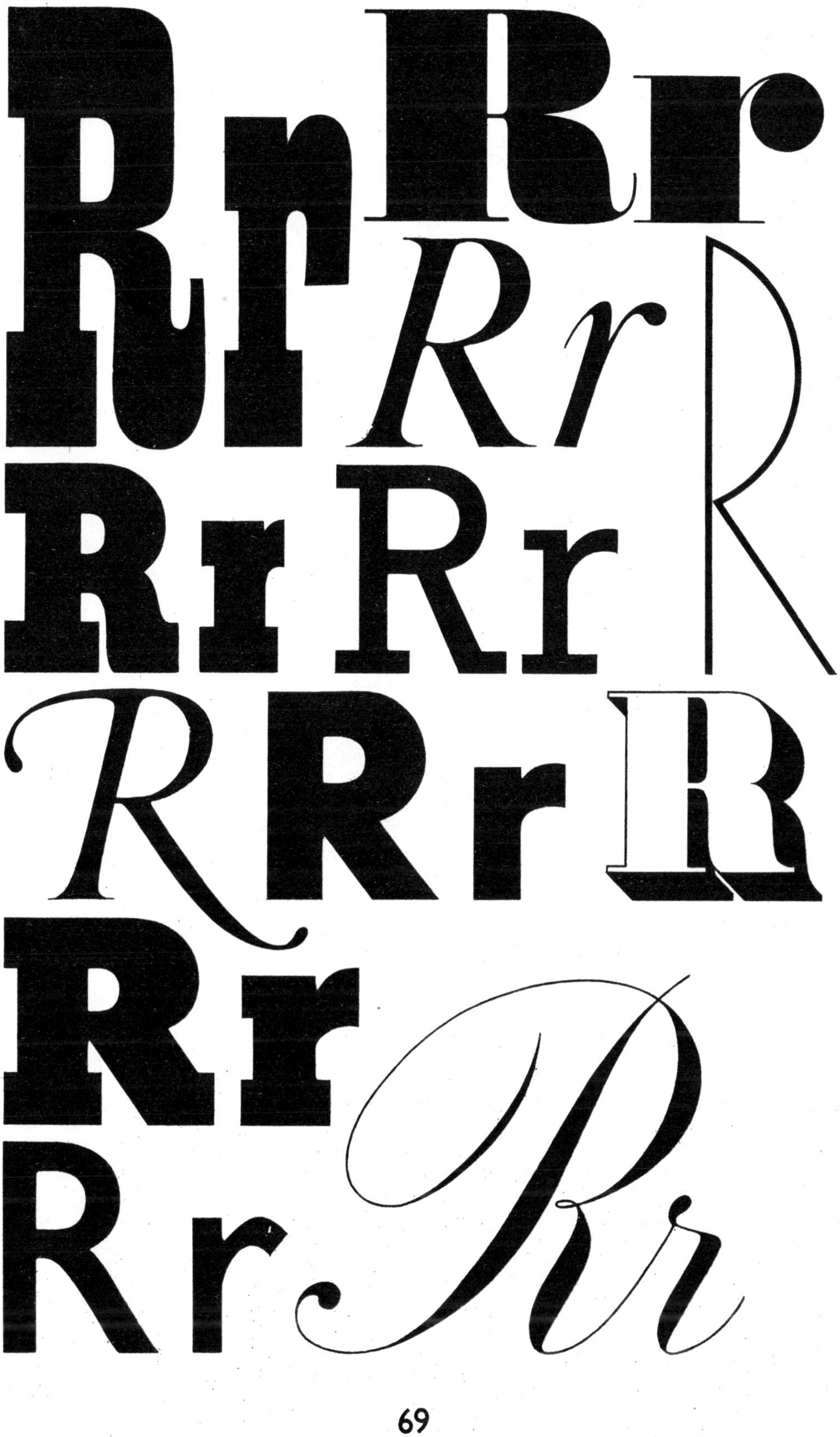

Rr Rr Rr
Rr Rr R
Rr R r
RR Rr
Rr R Rr

Rr Rr Rr
Rr Rr
R R R
Rr R kr
Rr Rr

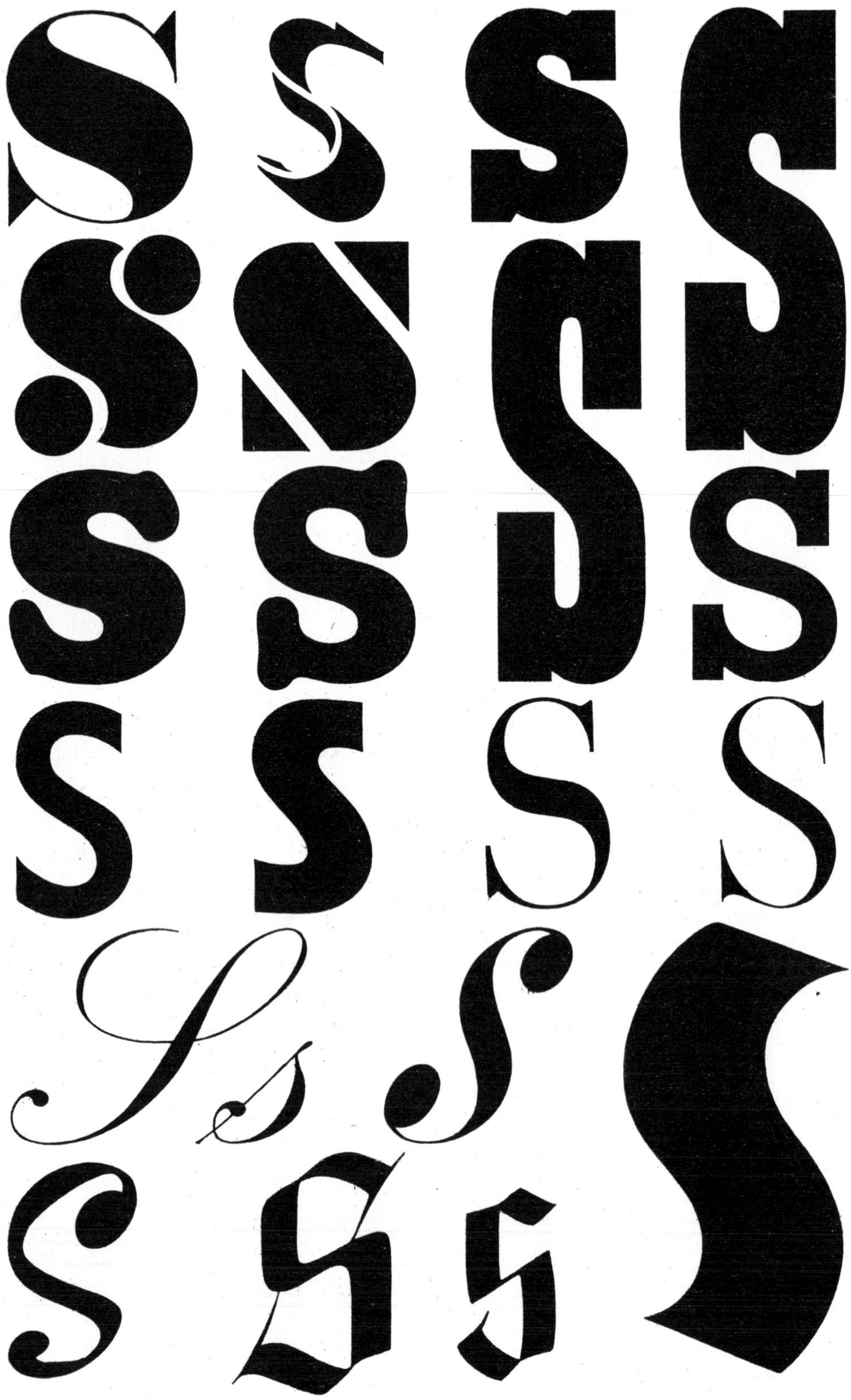

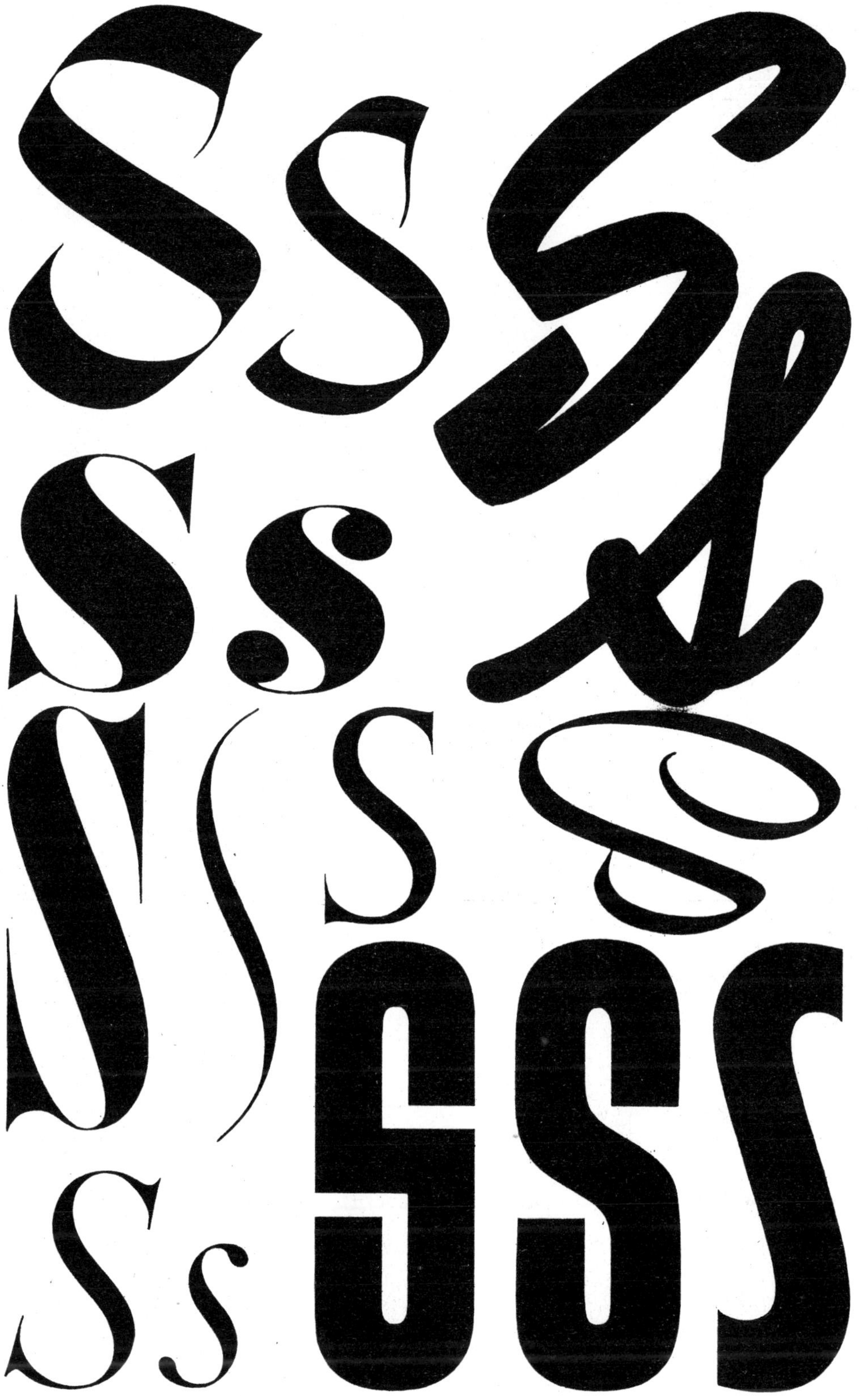

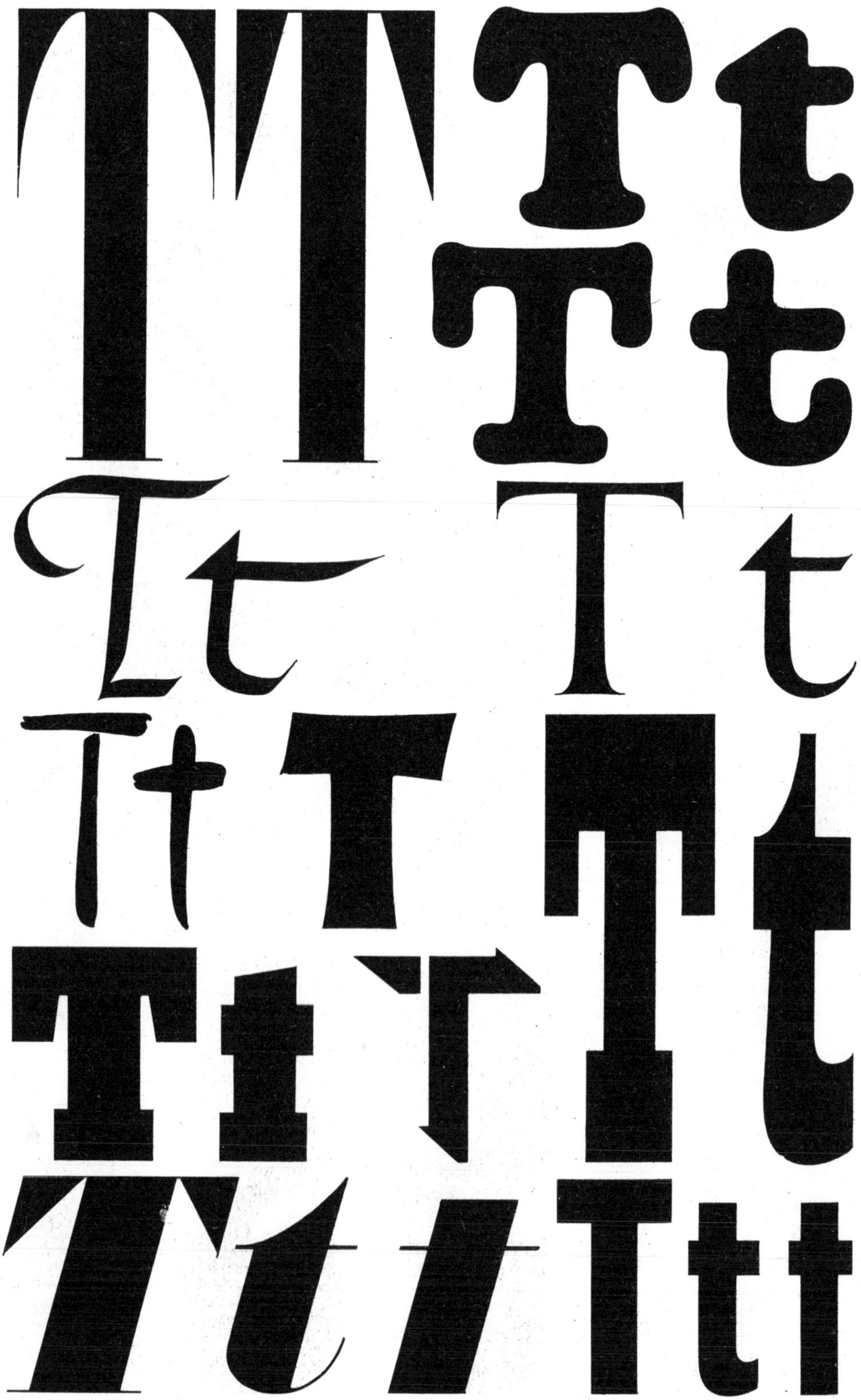

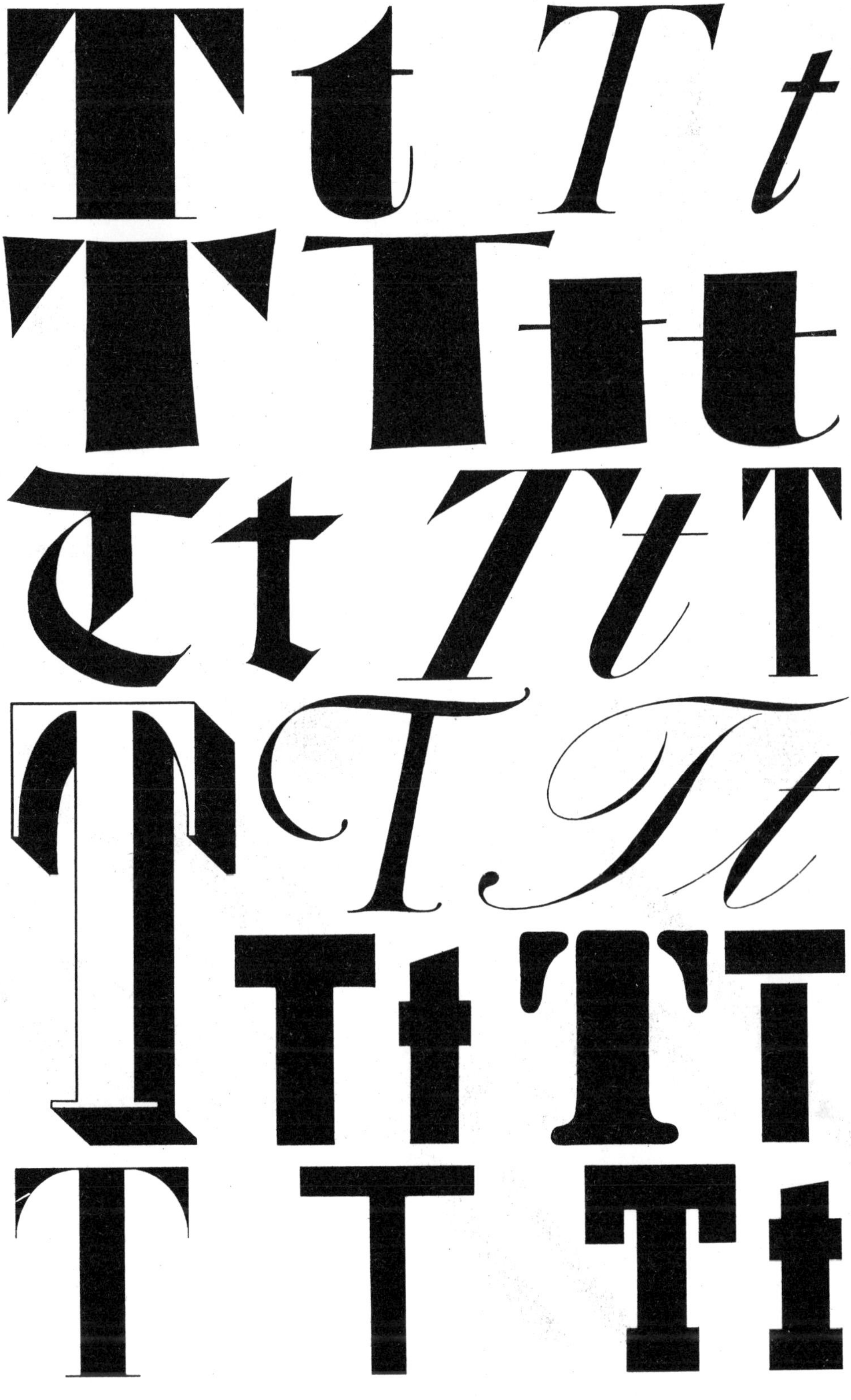

Tt TtTt
TtTt
Tt
Truffles

Ս Ս Ս Ս Ս Ս Ս Ս Ս ՍuՍu Ս Ս Ս Ս Ս u Ս ՍuՍ Ս u

Uu Uu Uu
Uu Uu Uu
Uu Uu Üu
Uu Uu Uu
Uu Uu Uu
Uu Uu Uu

Undies

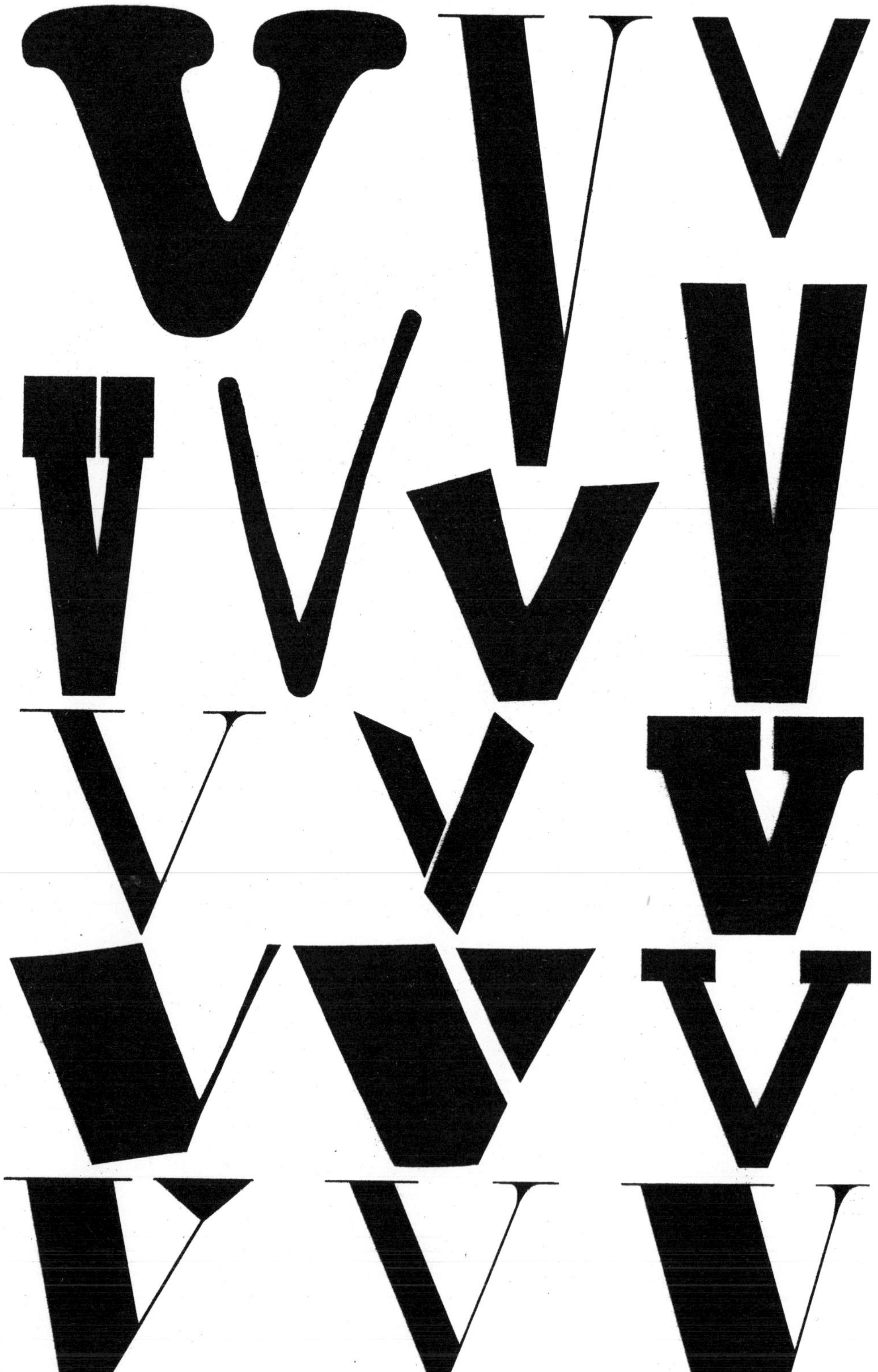

Velour

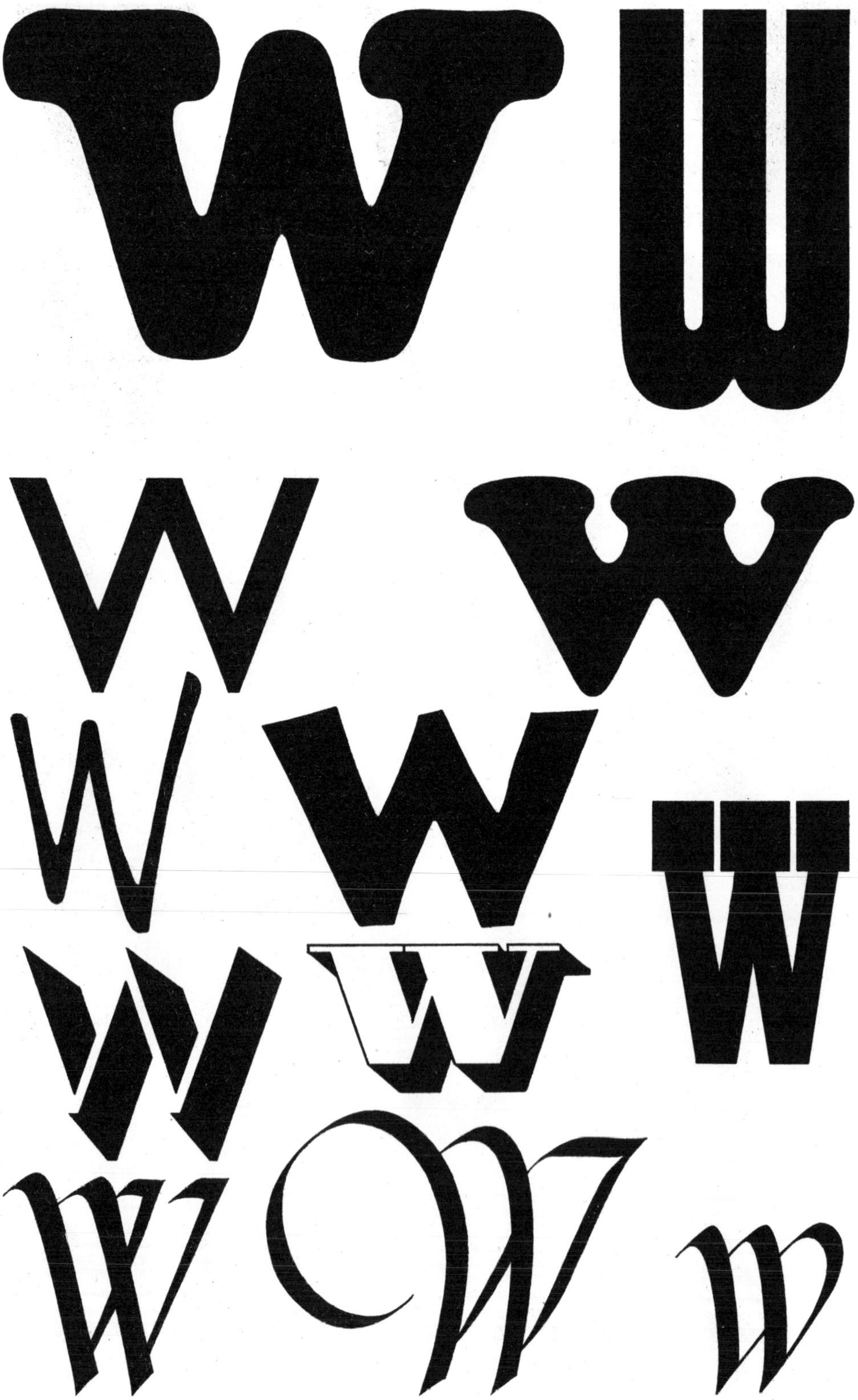

W W w
W W W
W W w
W a w
Winter in
Sunshine

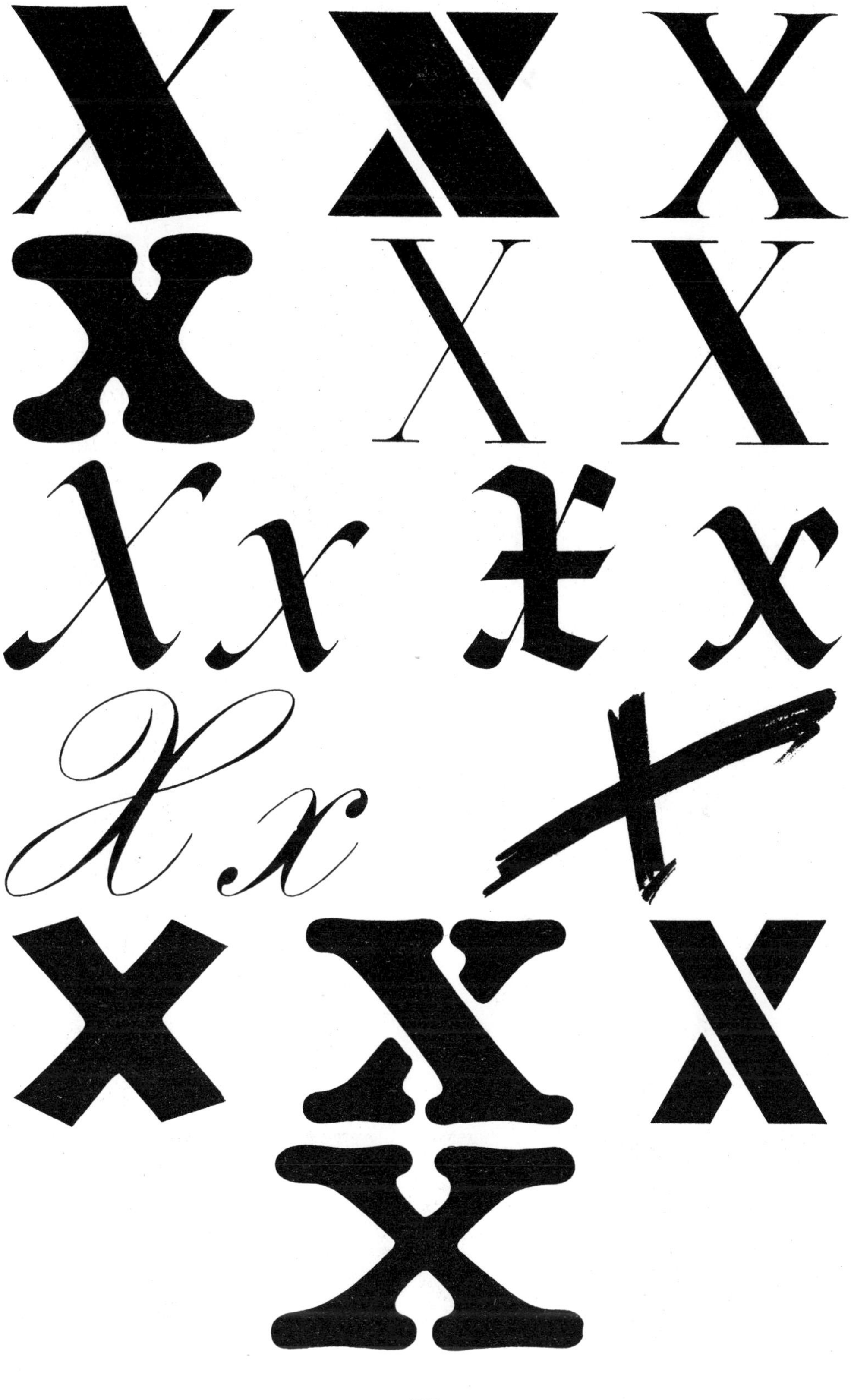

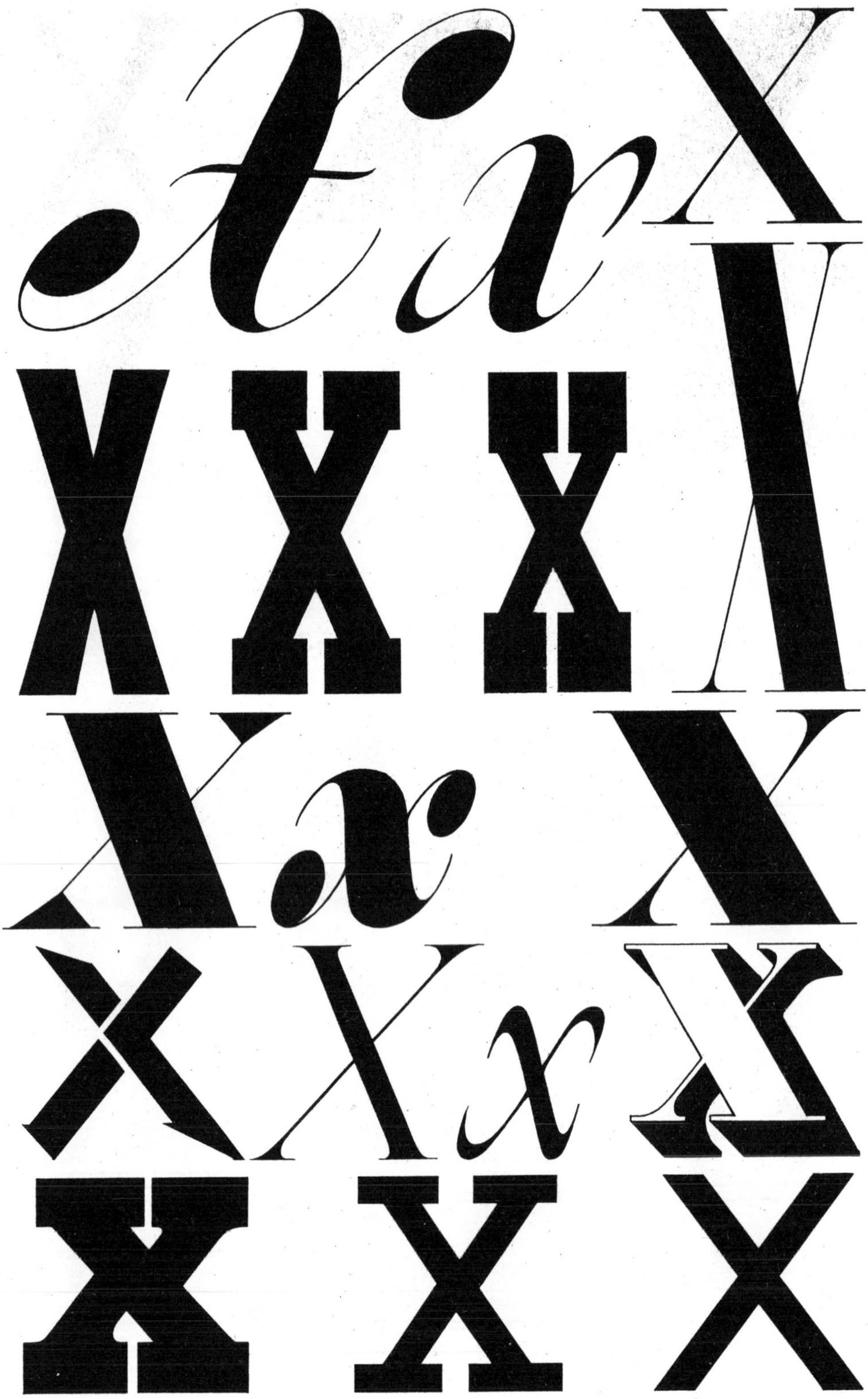

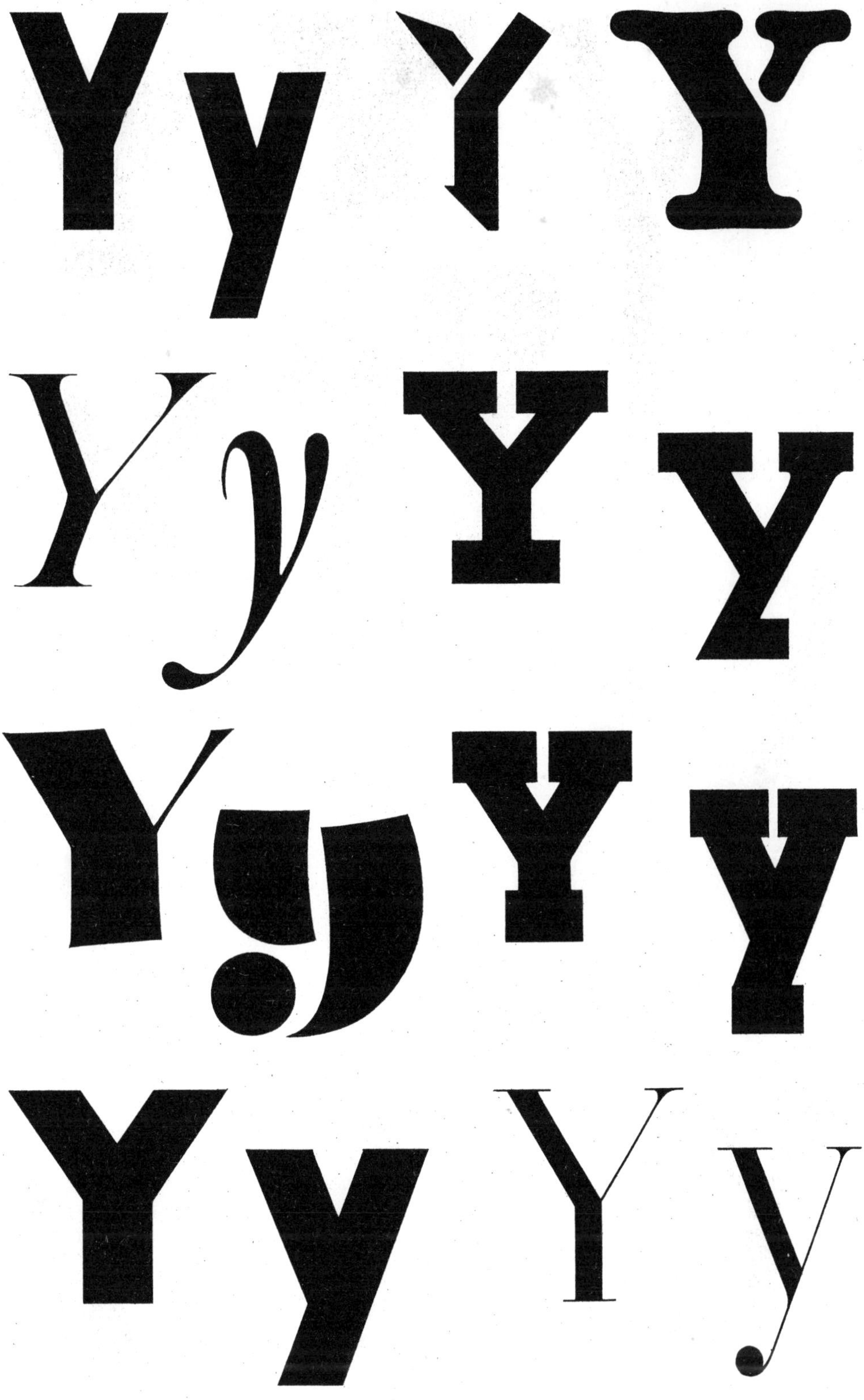

Yy Yy Yy

Yy Yy Yy

Yy Yy Yy

Yyyyyy

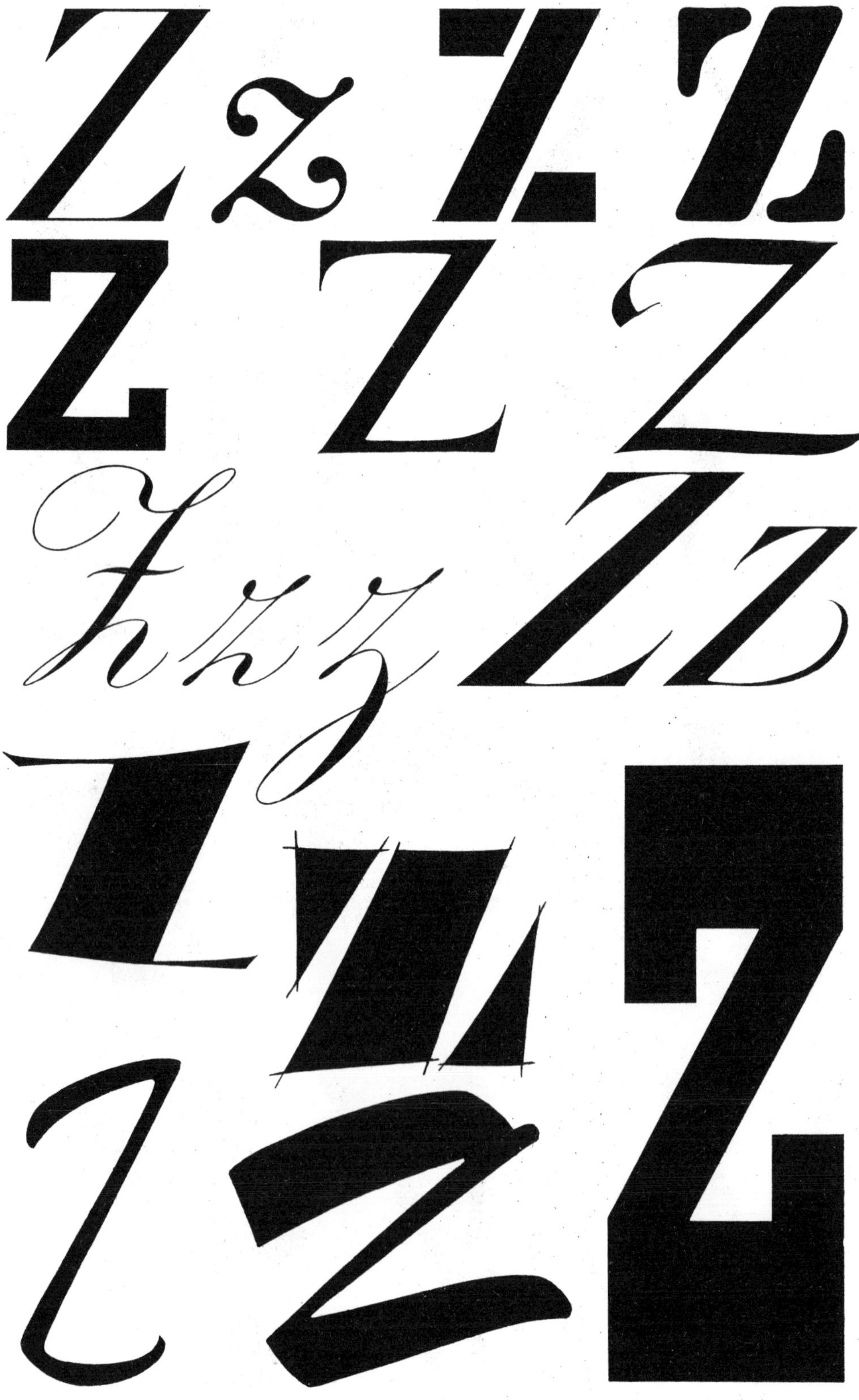